Communication and Culture:
An Introduction

COMMUNICATION
AND CULTURE:
An Introduction

edited by
Gunther Kress

Published by
NEW SOUTH WALES UNIVERSITY PRESS
PO Box 1 Kensington NSW Australia 2033
Telephone (02) 398 8900 Fax (02) 398 3408

First published in 1988
Reprinted in 1989 and 1993
Printed by Australian Print Group, Maryborough, Vic.

National Library of Australia
Cataloguing-in-Publication entry:

Communication and culture.

Bibliography.
Includes index.
ISBN 0 86840 266 4.

1. Communication. 2. Communication – Social aspects.
3. Mass media. 4. Mass media – Social aspects.
5. Social sciences. 1. Kress, Gunther, 1940–

302.2

CONTENTS

Communication and Culture   *Gunther Kress*

Communication □ Culture and Meaning □ Culture and Communication □ Ways of Thinking about Communication and Culture □ Further Reading □

Australian Society   *Ann Curthoys*

Concepts in Social Theory □ Capitalism and Industrialisation □ The Organisation of Work under Industrial Capitalism □ Class Gender □ Family and Kinship □ The State □

Australian History and Society □ The British Takeover □ Self-government and the Persecution of the Aboriginal Population □ The new Imperialism and 'The Commonwealth' □ Australia after the Second World War □ Governing Australia □ The Australian Nation: Immigration and Ethnic Diversity □ Further Reading □

GENERAL EDITOR'S PREFACE

Communication and Culture is the first in a series of books that will deal with the complex and topical area sketched in by the introductory title. Many books have been written and are constantly being published on the subject of Australian culture. They range from the concerns of political scientists to those of sociologists, journalists, art critics, or cultural historians. The aim of this series is to draw on and to extend such work, and to bring the related categories of culture and communication into a sharper focus as areas worthy of intensive attention in their own right. Australian society is extraordinarily complex and culturally diverse, with all the multitudinous and often intractable problems attendant on such diversity. In bringing that richness and diversity to our attention the series will make its contribution to solving the problems of equitable participation in processes of communication in our society.

Gunther Kress,
Dean,
Faculty of Humanities and Social Sciences,
New South Wales Institute of Technology

GENERAL EDITOR'S PREFACE
TO THE 3RD EDITION

Books, like other commodities, have their use-by dates. Just as the cream can go off, the butter rancid, or the biscuits stale, so books can exceed their shelf-life: they may be overtaken by new theoretical developments; or the state of affairs they initially dealt with may have changed beyond recognition; or they may simply drop out of fashion. **Communication and Culture** seems, however, to have kept its use for the readers for whom it was always intended, namely those interested in taking some first steps in the broad domain marked out by its title. It foregrounds a concern with describing and understanding crucial aspects of culture and communication, and it uses theory for that end, rather than foregrounding and concentrating on theory and theoretical niceties. That has meant that it has been more resistant to the swing of -isms than it would otherwise have been. Of course there have been theoretical changes since 1988. And there have been changes in the state of social, cultural and economic affairs in Australia, and nowhere more severely than in the media-industries. When the book was being written, through 1986 and 1987 the state of media ownership in Australia seemed a divinely ordained, eternal given with a legislative system of support engraved on tablets of stone.

As the book went into its first printing the certainties of that world collapsed; and it has been shifting since, changes not without certain ironic or amusing moments for those onlookers who have been able to retain vestiges of a sense of humour.

And while this has affected some of the details described in chapter 3, 'Communication as an industry', it has not altered in any fundamental sense the general theoretical framework outlined by Helen Wilson in that chapter. If I were freshly starting on this book now, in 1992, there are not many things I would want to change, or ask my co-writers to bear in mind. Personally I would now place a somewhat greater emphasis on the multi- and intercultural aspects which are having a fundamentally transforming effect even now on all aspects of

Australian society. I would now place greater emphasis on aspects of visual means of communication, for again it seems to me that Western technological societies are in the middle of a shift of an enormous magnitude, involving in the relative importance of verbal and visual modes of communication.

But these concerns are dealt with in the book, even if perhaps with somewhat less weight than I would want to give them now. I remain very satisfied with what the book is setting out to do: starting with considerations of central parts of social and cultural life, and forms of communication, developing ways of understanding these, and in that process developing more general and widely applicable ideas about this enormously important and absorbing field. I think it's fine for the book to stay out on the shelves for a little longer.

Gunther Kress,
Professor of Education,
Institute of Education,
University of London

September 1992.

CONTRIBUTORS

Anne Cranny-Francis is Senior Lecturer in the Department of English at the University of Wollongong. She has written on Australian literature, on nineteenth century literature and on popular fiction. She is the author of *Feminist Fictions* (Polity Press 1990) and *Engendered Fictions* (NSW University Press 1992).

Ann Curthoys is Professor of Social History at the University of Technology, Sydney. She has published articles and chapters in feminist theory and in Australian history, particularly in theories of the sexual division of labour; the history of women and work; racism, Aboriginal policy, and the anti-Chinese movements; the establishment of Australian television; and the post-1970 women's movement. She has co-edited several books (with John Merritt) *Better Dead than Red: Australia's First Cold War* (Allen and Unwin), and (with Allan Martin and Tim Rowse) *Australians since 1939* (Fairfax, Syme and Weldon). She is the author of *For and Against Feminism* (Allen and Unwin 1990).

Gunther Kress is Professor of English at the Institute of Education, University of London. He is interested in the broad areas of language and culture, and of literacies, including visual literacy. His more recent books include *Social Semiotics* (Polity Press 1988, with Bob Hodge), *Reading Images* (Deaken University Press 1990, with Theo van Leeuwen), and the re-publication of an extended version of *Language as Ideology* (Routledge 1992, with Bob Hodge).

Noel Sanders is Senior Lecturer in the School of Humanities at the University of Technology, Sydney. He teaches in the Communication degree, in Media Studies, Textual Studies and in various aspects of popular culture. He has published numerous articles in these areas. He is a published composer, whose works have been performed in concerts in Australia and New Zealand.

Helen Wilson is Senior Lecturer in the School of Humanities at the University of Technology, Sydney. She teaches in the Communication degree, in areas ranging from Radio to Textual Studies to Media Studies and Communication technology and policy. She has published numerous articles and chapters in these areas. She is co-author (with Bill Bonney) of *Australia's Commercial Media* (Macmillan 1983) and editor of *Public Communication* (Macmillan 1988). She has been actively involved with public radio station 2SER FM since its foundation in 1980.

PREFACE

The study of culture and the study of communication each has its own long history. Such work has been conducted under labels as various as poetry, philosophy, classics, literature, sociology, history, anthropology, grammar and rhetoric, psychology, in branches of anthropology such as the ethnography of communications, in drama, in linguistics, and in many others. In more recent times, over the last two decades particularly, each of the two has come much more into its own right so that there are now courses in tertiary institutions called 'cultural studies' and 'communication studies', sometimes joined as 'communication and cultural studies'.

The reasons for that development are various, but are connected with broad social and cultural changes. Academic disciplines are an integral part of those complex social and cultural processes to which we give, in hindsight, the name history. For instance, there was nothing arbitrary about the fact that at the beginning of this century a new discipline called 'English' developed, displacing from their place of prominence both classics and philosophy. That change had to do, among other things, with the rise of the public service, particularly in the United Kingdom, and, more broadly, with the spread of white-collar work and the concomitant need for a workforce well trained in the uses of the vernacular. All academic disciplines have their histories, and all of them are closely enmeshed in the complex cultural histories of particular societies.

Cultural studies and communication studies are no exception. The recent emergence of each is not the result of the whim of a few academics in their ivory towers — academics, alas, do not have that kind of power! The study of culture in the form of 'exotic' cultures had been the domain of anthropology. The emergence of cultural studies as the attempt to discover cultural diversity within the one society coincides precisely with the final period of disintegration of the British colonial empire (and of European colonial empires) in the mid fifties. In imperial days the gaze of the (European) anthropologist was fixed on the inhabitants of distant shores and on the 'exotic' products of their activities. By displaying the strangeness of foreign cultures the homogeneity of the home culture could be constantly confirmed, in fact, was never called into question.

Now, political contingency meant that that gaze had to turn inward, and here it discovered the exotic within the boundaries of the nation: the working class, the mods and rockers; later on, women, blacks. The academic spotlight, always emanating and directed from positions of relatively greater power, could now be turned on those groups with lesser power within the same society.

The emergence of cultural studies in Australia did follow British leads. But here too, it received a mighty twin impetus. On the one hand, it came from the social and political problem brought about by two decades of non-Anglo immigration. And on the other hand, it came from an increasingly urgent realisation that the internal colonialism practised towards Australia's Aboriginal people could no longer be sustained in that form. The pressing need to come to terms with the effects of more than a century and a half of oppression and dispossession of the Aboriginal people, together with the facts of multiculturalism could, by the late sixties to early seventies, no longer be ignored. It had become a social and political issue, a problem of the largest scale. Although these links are never direct, the fact that Australia could no longer be thought about — or perhaps even governed — as a culturally homogeneous nation gave enormous impetus to the development of cultural studies in Australia.

The history of communication studies is no less tied into real social issues. The rapid development of information technologies, the massive spread of the electronic media, the quantum leap in the size of the so-called service sector, all call for a kind of education that is not being provided by the traditional academic disciplines. Each of them deals with aspects of the kinds of knowledges and skills called for: literature with the analysis of complex texts; psychology with the behaviour of people in interactions; sociology with the structures and processes of groups; linguistics with the structure of language; fine arts with aesthetic aspects of texts and communication. None of them provides the range and particular combination of knowledge and skill needed in this new social and economic situation. In other words, a particular social and economic problem has arisen as the result of economic, social and technological changes, and a new area of study is needed to address and deal with the problem. Communication studies incorporates many of the concerns of other disciplines but combines them in particular ways, in addition to introducing new concerns — such as an interest in technology, social change, and their effects on the structures and contents of communication. Above all, Communication studies is oriented towards the study of all social behaviour as meaningful action, and of the products of all such meaningful actions as organised by codes and expressed, essentially, in the form of *texts*. While literature focuses on the verbal code and literary texts, communication studies takes as its object of study texts that consist of verbal, visual, and aural codes — television advertisements for instance. And while literature is defined by its interest in a range of texts defined as 'beautiful', 'aesthetically valuable', communication studies operates without a prior system of valuation. It concerns itself with the whole range of cultural codes: of dress, furnishing, gesture, language; and it deals equally with all media, from verbal language to photography, textiles, bricks, food — in fact any medium through which the meanings of a culture find their expression.

This book is meant as an introduction for those who are interested in the range of things indicated by those encompassing labels, communication and culture: whether as the proverbial interested layperson, as an intending student of a formal course, or as someone who has just started such a course and would like a broad and relatively non-technical perspective on that whole area. The book is quite deliberately non-academic — its writers weren't too fussed about preserving the complex etiquette or the boundaries of the various disciplines. It isn't a heavily theoretical book, rather it focuses on issues; and where it does bring in theory, it does so as a means for getting somewhere with a particular problem. The book sketches in those features of the landscape that are crucial for getting a first bearing: an introduction to the history and present structure of one society; a sketch of the lay of the land of the major institutions in the mass media; an indication of how to begin thinking about what the media produce; and a focus on the two basic codes of verbal language and visual images. It will succeed if it whets the appetite, and points to other eateries!

As editor I would like to make a few brief acknowledgements. I enjoyed working with my co-writers on this project. I have benefited from the work of many of my colleagues, and from the enthusiasm and insight of the students with whom I have worked — benefited in ways that are later often invisible to oneself, but which leave their effects everywhere. Rachel Kress did a consumer test of sections of this book for me, and I would like to thank her for that. Kurt Brereton gave me his expert help in the preparation of images, for which I am most grateful. I have had the benefit of constant access to a sympathetic and unremittingly perceptive reader in Jill Brewster. Many formulations and reworkings of my part of this enterprise are due to her. She gave me substantial material help in the preparation of this book. This acknowledgement is a small token of my thanks to her.

HOW TO READ THIS BOOK

All texts are constructed by their producers with a particular kind of reader in mind, and therefore suggest a particular 'reading' also. Texts are constructed so as to position the reader in a quite specific way. For instance, a piece of reporting in the financial pages of a newspaper might attempt to place us as readers in the position where we accept, without any hesitation or question, a set of values or attitudes towards the economy, as helpless and anxious victims, or as responsible actors. A good text, from the producer's point of view, has an appearance of naturalness about it; it will appear obvious to its readers. The text of this book is no exception. So the very first thing that an aware reader needs to do is to look for the constructedness of the text, to ask how, in what way, to what ends the text is positioning her/him. When I issue my seemingly innocuous instruction on how to read, you should be on your guard at once. What am I trying to achieve? Well, I think that what I'm trying to achieve is at least the following: to give you one way of reading the book — my preferred reading for you; to make you aware of my action, both for now and for all of your future reading; and to make you think that I'm very open about this, putting my cards on the table and letting *you* make the decision.

Having given you fair warning, I'll now proceed. This book can be read in a number of ways, and for different purposes. You might like to read it from beginning to end, merely for interest. It says things of interest on the subject of communication, on culture, and on Australian culture. That seems to me to be a worthwhile reading. You might like to focus on particular chapters: for instance to get an understanding of how images work, perhaps so you can become a better reader of images, or perhaps so you can learn to construct images even more cunningly. All the chapters provide both general information and insights into particular areas, and also a means of analysis and description of specific areas of communication. Each of the chapters can stand on its own, though they do proceed from relatively simple to quite complex arguments by a gradual building up of concepts in an overall framework.

I have organised the chapters of the book so as to place a description of Australia's society and its history very early, as the second chapter.

That conforms with the view I will be putting forward in the following chapter which is shared by all the writers of this book, namely that any discussion of communication can only make sense if we understand the context — the sets of values, the practices, the potent meanings of a culture. Such an understanding must, in my view, rest on a sense of the culture and the society as it is now, how it has come to be where it is, and what it is. That allows us then to see why certain things are talked about, how they're talked about, who can say what to whom, who has access to what meanings, and who has access to the means for the dissemination of meanings.

In taking this starting point the book is unusual. Books that deal with the subject of communication tend to start with discussions of theories of communication, or with examples of instances of communication. But in a view in which culture and communication are seen as different aspects of the same subject matter, the starting point must be the description of the society and the culture in which communication takes place. It is there, after all, where meanings originate and are constantly made, in the processes of cultural production and in the processes of communication.

Hence the ordering of the book. Following on a general and, I hope, gentle introduction to the twin concepts of communication and culture, is a chapter on Australian society, its structure and its history. This is followed in Chapter Three by the exploration of one aspect of that social structure and of the economy, the communication industries. The next two chapters deal with two kinds of codes: the verbal codes of language, speech and writing; and visual codes, mainly painting and photography. Their respective ordering is not intended to have any particular significance. My own view, governed by my interest in language, is that language is the most fully articulated cultural code of all; certainly it is the most intensively studied, and it has provided ways of thinking about the structure and organisation of other cultural codes, visual codes included. Of course very many of the texts we encounter in our experience of culture are composites of verbal and visual codes — and frequently of others as well: films, videos, hoardings, advertisements, books, comics, magazines, rockclips, streetscapes, posters. Therefore we need a working and useable understanding of the complex interaction of the various codes in any one message. That is provided in the final chapter, which deals with media products that are most complex in their production, composition, reception and effects, namely film and video.

At the beginning of each chapter I have provided a brief piece, which is meant to suggest one reading of the chapter; I hope it may be helpful to a reader who is quite new to this area. There is a brief glossary of major terms used in the book; the definitions are based largely on the discussion in the relevant section. There are other and more extensive glossaries available, which may differ in their definitions. I hope the major aid to reading the book will be the index, which is deliberately quite detailed. The best way to get a sense of the meaning of a term is to read around in the context where it is used.

That is my rationale for the structuring of this book, and the kind of reading that that suggests: an understanding of culture as the fundamental prerequisite for an understanding of communication. You may find interest in that; you may also wish to read against that structure and make *your* sense of this book, out of a dialogue of your purposes and your order and those of the writers of this book. For now, I'll issue no further instructions.

CHAPTER ONE

▼

Communication and Culture

by
Gunther Kress

There is a still strongly persistent tradition which separates the study of communication from the study of culture. Handbooks still proliferate telling their readers how to communicate (better), and put forward little boxes of verbal or non-verbal tricks which never seem to have any relation to cultural settings. Culture on the other hand is, within that tradition, still the provenance either of anthropology — as a species of the exotic — or the provenance of the purveyors of high culture to a social elite. In this book the two are brought together as two entirely interconnected aspects of the one phenomenon, namely that of meaning. Culture is the domain of meaningful human activity and of its effects and resultant objects; communication is the domain of the intended or unintended exchange of meanings between social/cultural agents. The processes of communication produce meanings; cultural production brings into existence meaningful objects, which in their turn communicate their meanings. The concept of meaning therefore inextricably links these two aspects of the one domain.

Over the last decade or so this conjunction has gained increasing currency due, in a very large part, to the labours of a group of intellectuals in Britain. Among these particular mention should be made of Raymond Williams, and of a group of scholars working at the Centre for Contemporary Cultural Studies in the University of Birmingham. As a result of their work there exist now some detailed, subtle and theoretically highly developed accounts of a range of cultural phenomena. This introductory chapter aims not at any theoretical sophistication, but rather intends to describe and establish the inevitable links of communication and culture in an accessible fashion, and to provide the outline of a comprehensive yet simple model of the communication process.

Communication

'Communication', the idea, perhaps even the activity, is a matter of great public interest. We know that ours is the information age, where everything depends on communication. Papers and politicians, marriage counsellors and media pundits all tell us that our problems are really due to bad communication. And so communication itself is a big industry. It employs not only people like myself who write about it, but countless experts who try to fix communication problems. There are 'communication and awareness weekends' to 'put you in touch with yourself' — for those who can pay, at least. Countless short courses are run in industry, in the public service, in commerce, and of course by educational institutions. Most jobs now demand demonstrable skills in communication. Promotion in a job depends on it, and great value is attached to someone's level of skill in oral or written communication. 'Being a great communicator' seems to be the highest accolade that can be paid to a president of the United States of America. Economic productivity would definitely increase if we could only improve it, the output of each worker would shoot up; for, after all, aren't most problems in industrial relations caused by the lack of it?

If communication is so important, what is it? Well, on the one level it is a word: 'communication'. That word is a noun, and nouns give object-like meanings to what they name. So 'communication' is object-like; it seems to be a thing, like the broom in the cupboard, or the trade balance. But while you can sweep the floor with a broom, you can't do anything much with communication. You can try to improve it, tinker with it, or bemoan it; and to that extent it is a bit like the trade balance. The point is that while communication is a noun, it is a name not for an object, but for a process, and a very complex process at that. I don't particularly wish to give a definition of communication here, rather I would like to point to some things we need to bear in mind either when thinking and talking about it, or when doing it. For the rest I would much prefer to let the different chapters in the book do that slow but necessary job of building up and filling in the picture bit by bit.

To say that communication is a process is to say that it involves a range of activities, aspects and participants. Cutting, for instance, is also a process. It involves: an instrument, the knife; someone to use the instrument, the 'cutter'; something to cut — the cloth, the loaf of bread, or the string; quite often someone for whom the action is performed — 'Could you cut me another slice, please?' and always a purpose — '. . . because I'd like to get up the rest of this delicious gravy'. Raymond Williams says (in *Keywords*) in an entry under 'Communication' that during the nineteenth century the meaning of the word included and referred mainly to the physical means of communication, 'lines of communication', such as roads, canals, railways. In the later part of that century, with 'the development of other means of passing information and maintaining social contact *Communications* came also and perhaps predominantly to refer to such MEDIA as the press and broadcasting' (62-63).

While, as he says, 'communications is now usually used for (the transmission of) information and ideas' (63), there is still a sense of the concreteness of that earlier use in much of our thinking about communication. Indeed the major model in communication theory could be taken to be a metaphor of nineteenth century transport. That model has three components — the sender (S), the message (M), and the receiver (R) — linked in a unidirectional way: S→ M → R. This is much like a Leeds textile manufacturer (S) might have thought about sending a bale of cloth (M) in a barge on the Leeds–Liverpool canal to a merchant (R) in Liverpool.

Later in this chapter I will describe an alternative way of thinking about communication in some detail. At the moment I want to emphasise a few general points. First, communication is about meaning rather than about information. By making that distinction I wish to include matters such as attitudes, social relations, individual feelings, social positioning of sender and receiver, as well as those things normally thought of as information — statements about the physical and social world. In other words, everything that has cultural significance enters into communication in the sense in which the word is used in this book. Second, communication is about the production and consumption of meaning in actual processes of communication. Therefore attention will need to be paid to consumers of meaning and to their acitivity in this process as much as to producers of meaning. Third, the processes of communication take place in a socially and culturally formed world. Hence communication never involves 'just' individuals expressing 'their' meanings. The meanings are produced and consumed by individuals who are already socially and culturally formed, and who draw on the meanings of their culture and social group. Fourth, the processes of communication are much more and other than the 'sharing of meaning', or the 'mutual construction of meaning'. Societies consist of multiplicities of social and cultural groupings, and interactions between and across such groupings are as likely to involve contradiction and contestation as they are to involve 'sharing'. In fact, sharing is a most unlikely candidate as a notion to explain the processes of communication; after all, once we have shared all our meanings what is there left to talk about? What motive or possibility remains for sharing once everything has been shared? So, fifth and last, the processes of communication are likely to be based on difference *and* on the resolution of difference at one and the same time.

To the nice, friendly· definition of communication as a sharing of meaning, as mutual meaning-making, we would certainly need to add some more hard-edged and realistic notions. For instance, the ideas that the processes of communication can have the effect of becoming devices of control, or means of instruction, or suppression. A teacher in the class-room who says 'Ok, open your books on page 132 now; Susie, start read-ing . . .', is using certain linguistic forms in order to exercise power and control the activities of the class. An article in a newspaper on 'Your first job interview' is giving me (if I am an appropriate reader) instructions on what to do, how to behave, who and how to be. And traffic signs give me quite precise instructions — if I understand the Highway Code — on what I may and may not do.

The point is that the processes of communication always take place in a specific social and cultural setting, never simply between you and me just as individuals; and the structures of power, of authority, as well as the structures of solidarity, exert their influence on the participants.

Culture and Meaning

As a child I remember going with my grandmother in early spring to her allotment on the edge of the small town. There was great activity; every-one was pulling out old vegetables, hoeing, raking, measuring, drilling holes for seeds. Some weeks later the scene and the activities had changed. Neat rows of seedlings, symmetrically spaced, had appeared, and the people were now transplanting, weeding, watering. And so it would go into the season, with changes in the weather, the scene and the activities. To me, then, all that activity and all the changes seemed entirely natural, ordinary and quite unremarkable. As I reflect on it now it seems to me a most fitting metaphor for the description of culture and cultural activity, and of the relation of nature and culture. Nature pro-vided the ground (literally) on which culture could work: the soil, the seeds, the weather, the water. The decision, however, to place the allot-ments on the southern edge of the town was an entirely cultural matter, as was the size of each allotment (or the very concept of an allotment!). Culture, too, had its effect on what kinds of tools would be used: forks and spades, hoes and rakes of certain kinds, dibble-sticks, balls of string and sticks to mark the rows, and so on. Culture determined how wide the paths between the beds should be, and how high above the path the level of the bed. Of course it was a matter of culture too what seeds were available and would be sown and in what proportion — related to habits of eating, which were themselves expressions of notions of nutrition, connected to class, and to ideas of what was 'proper'. It would have seemed a transgression of an inexcusable kind to my grandmother to have given over too much space in her garden to luxury vegetables such as early lettuces and cucumbers, at the expense of growing early potatoes. She had of course a very real reason: potatoes provided more nutrition for her family at a lesser cost of time than lettuces or cucumbers. Lettuces and cucumbers later in the season — in June, July and August — were fine; then they needed relatively little attention. So notions of social class emerged not only in *what* we ate, but at what time in the year we ate it. Eating lettuce in April was a luxury and meant either reprehensible extravagance and profligacy, or membership of the upper classes.

Culture, then, is the result and effect of human action on nature, the transformation of nature through the culturally guided activity of human beings. In this it is important to bear in mind the place of the individual agent, in the double role of the actor who works on nature and the bearer of cultural values. To my childish eye all the allotments looked the same, and it used to be my constant worry how to find our allotment when I was sent there by myself. The effect of culture had been to produce plots that reproduced abstract and complex patterns in nearly identical and concrete material form everywhere. Yet the adults, fully competent in their culture, attended not so much to cultural similarity, but to individual difference and variation; they had no difficulty in going straight to their plot.

The interaction of culture and nature is a complex one. Nature sets the ground and furnishes the materials, culture performs the transformations of that ground and the materials. The transformations themselves are constrained by nature. Weather directed when the planting and sowing would begin; soil type influenced the tools that were used, and climate determined what could be grown. Working too much against nature, that is, exaggerating culture, involved greater costs in human energy and time — through the need for 'hot-beds' or greenhouses for instance. Working too much with nature, underplaying culture, involved costs of a different sort; it might mean doing without the pleasure and rewards of culture — eating what would grow naturally ('weeds') — with the consequent nutritional limitations. Yet within the constraints set by nature, culture made its own rules. In Germany, men and women both worked in the allotments; when I saw allotments again, in northern England some twenty years later, I was struck by the fact that allotments were the exclusive domain of men. And while English allotments had some similarities they also looked a lot different from German Schrebergärten; their produce too was very different.

It is in the area where culture can and does set its own rules that meaning is made. In that area every action is significant, and the effects of all actions have meaning. Within culture all actions are made in the context of the possibility of other choices of action: growing early lettuces rather than potatoes; growing this range of vegetables and fruits rather than that; not planting in neat rows; growing some flowers in the allotment, and so on. It is that possibility of choice, the choice itself and sometimes the deviation from the system of choices, that makes human cultural activity meaningful. The products and objects resulting from these actions bear the meanings of their prior activities and the choices that were made.

Cultural artefacts are therefore more than simply objects. A garden fork speaks of a particular way of preparing soil and growing things, that is, of a particular mode of relating to nature. It speaks of a certain kind of technology (wood versus steel, manual versus mechanical). It is therefore an object that carries meaning, it is a *sign* much in the way that the word 'communication' is a sign. And like the sign/word, the sign/tool is part of a whole system of signs: spade, rake, dibble-stick, string, gardening knife, watering-can, fork. Each carries meaning as a sign, and the total system of tool/signs carries a complex of meanings about one particular area of culture, namely gardening. The system tells us about the relation of human beings to nature, about their relation to each other in social organisations.

In a cultural view a spade is therefore a lot more than a spade. A spade can tell us about a whole system of meaning and significance. But the spade can also be turned back on nature, like all cultural objects. When culture turns back on nature (rather than 'just' working on nature), then nature becomes drawn into culture and into cultural meaning. From the point of view of the spade — or better, of the user of the spade — the earth, the soil, is defined in terms of the tool: easy to dig, hard to dig, cloggy, soft, crumbly, too wet, too dry and dusty. The earth is drawn into a net of labels that reflect the cultural purposes of the gardener, who in time comes to see soil only in terms that make sense to a gardener and to the demands of growing crops. Nature, in its 'natural form' recedes and is replaced by a set of culturally determined labels that come to guide, shape, perhaps determine our thinking. To a farmer, for instance, nature has a quite particular look. Take, as a small example, the following extract from a highschool textbook in Geography:

Tropical savanna pastoral region

The environmental conditions of this region mean that it is poorly suited to most forms of agriculture. It receives most of its rainfall during the summer monsoons, and then experiences a winter drought. Furthermore, the natural savanna woodlands vegetation and grasslands have few nutrients for intensive grazing, the soils are poor, the region is a long distance from markets, and transport facilities are poorly developed. Thus, the land is used for little else except extensive beef cattle grazing on farms which sometimes exceed 15,000 square kilometres in size. The large size of the farm is needed because of the land's poor carrying capacity, which may mean one beast needs 20 to 30 hectares to survive. Attempts were made to establish irrigation agriculture around the Ord River in the 1960s, but saline soils, high costs of long distance transport to markets, and the costs of dam and irrigation canal construction led to the virtual failure of the scheme in the early 1970s. It was intended to produce cotton, sugar cane and rice in the Ord River Scheme. Another land use, mining, is now of greater value than beef grazing. Important minerals include uranium (Rum Jungle, Ranger, Nabarlek), bauxite (Weipa, Mitchell Plateau), iron ore (Yampi Sound, Frances Creek), manganese (Groote Eylandt), copper, lead, silver, zinc (all at Mount Isa) and gold (Tennant Creek). The largest towns in the region are Darwin and Mount Isa, each with just over 35,000 people.

(S.B. & D.M. Codrington, *World of Contrasts: Case Studies in World Development for Secondary Geography*, William Brooks, Sydney, 1982, p193.)

Clearly nature is viewed here from a very specific cultural point of view, namely that of primary industry — farming and mining. The labelling, the definition of nature, proceeds from that standpoint: the land 'is poorly suited to most forms of agriculture', has 'few nutrients for intensive grazing', and is 'a long distance from markets . . . Thus, 'the land is used for little else except extensive beef grazing . . .'. Another cultural viewpoint might be that of an environmentalist and conservationist group. Their description would differ markedly. A very different culture, that of the original Aboriginal inhabitants for example, would have a description of the land bearing no relation at all to the one given here.

These differences derive from the use made by different cultures of that space that is not determined by nature, where there is the possibility of a choice of differing kinds of actions on nature, different sets of transformations of nature. In these actions and transformations, constantly repeated over very long periods, nature is assimilated into culture, so that it becomes difficult or even impossible to see and think of nature 'as it really is'. All our approaches to nature are guided by that extensive frame of cultural valuations. We know that there is nature 'as such', a non-cultural reality, but we can't see what it is. In trying to see what kind of working and re-working cultural processes have performed on nature, nothing is more revealing than to contrast and compare different cultures. Even my modest and homely example of the allotment provides some insights. For instance, no-one can fail to be struck by the northern English penchant for growing enormously fat leeks. Anyone who has been to an agricultural show in Australia must wonder what the point of growing monstrously large pumpkins might be. And anyone who has seen German allotments is left wondering whether such neatness is absolutely essential for productive gardens. The answer, in my view, is the same in the three cases. Particular features are focused on and become highly significant and potent symbols in a culture, and into these symbols a whole range of complex meanings is condensed: about masculinity, about fecundity, about social order.

We don't have to wander to far-off lands and so-called exotic cultures in order to do this kind of comparative analysis. Any culture is as 'exotic' as any other; and those cultural differences existing within the one society are a quite sufficient ground for exploration. Look at the kinds of front gardens people have, in one street or in different suburbs. Look at fashions of dress among differing (sub) cultural groups, and the rapidly changing fashions adopted and adapted by social groups, particularly by young people; or consider how people furnish their houses, the kinds of food they eat, the way they structure their meals. And then consider how all these different systems fit together to make up complex wholes — say of a group of young people living in an inner city suburb, who dress in particular ways, eat certain kinds of food and furnish their rooms in their particular ways.

My description of the meaning of culture has moved several steps from the example of the allotment. When we consider the systems of fashion we are considering a system where culture (in the form of fashion) has worked on culture (in the form of clothing). Much of what we experience as cultural life is constructed at this kind of remove; it is the experience of the workings of culture on already complex cultural systems. Most of what we think of as culture is therefore at a very great remove from nature. Indeed, our conceptions of what is quintessentially cultural are of systems of that kind: architecture, clothing, food, literature, music, 'art' generally, the professions, and so on. To speculate for a moment. It may be that we can distinguish different cultural 'ages' by focusing on the relation of culture to nature that is dominant in a particular period. If the pre-industrial age is characterised by a fairly direct relation of culture working on nature (primary industry), the industrial age is marked by a somewhat more remote relation of nature and culture, culture working on the results of culture working on nature (secondary industry). The information age is then that period in which culture works entirely on objects that are themselves cultural products, to produce that new commodity 'information'.

In *Keywords* Raymond Williams provides a detailed history of the word in European usage and he distinguishes three current senses of the word: '(i) the independent and abstract noun that describes a general process of intellectual, spiritual and aesthetic development, from C18; (ii) the independent noun, whether used generally or specifically, that indicates a particular way of life, whether of the people, a period or a group, from Herder and C19. But we have also to recognise (iii) the independent and abstract noun that describes the works and practices of intellectual and especially artistic activity. This seems often now the most widespread use: *culture* is music, literature, painting and sculpture, theatre and film' (p.80). In this book the major part of my discussion (the allotment!) and the sense in which the word will generally be used is the second sense, which includes the more narrow usage of (iii). However, it is important to note that it is the third sense that tends to dominate in 'commonsense' discussions of the topic. When people say — or used to say — that 'Australia is a cultural desert', that is or was the sense being invoked. It has given rise to the identification of culture with high culture, and a consequent dismissal or overlooking, and certainly an undervaluing, of all other cultural practices and objects.

Culture and Communication

All cultural practices are significant, and all cultural objects are endowed with meaning. Hence it follows that everything cultural communicates. Every cultural practice is a communicative event. Every act of communication is a cultural event. The structures, processes and contents of communication are given by culture. Nothing outside culture can be a part of communication. Culture sets the ground entirely for communication, for what can be communicated, what is communicable, and for how it is communicated. On the one hand, anything outside the scope of communication is non-cultural. On the other hand, as communication is a cultural process, new cultural meanings are constantly produced in the processes of communication.

Culture and communication are two sides of the same coin. They are different labels designed to name different aspects of the same complex set of structures and processes. 'Culture' is the label that refers to the set of practices that produce meanings and to the resultant objects of those practices. It refers to human engagement in those practices, and to their effect on human beings acting together as a cultural group, as a 'culture'. 'Communication' is the label that refers to those meanings, and their conscious or unconscious, deliberate or accidental exchange among members of a culture, or among members of closely connected cultural groupings — in society. Like all exchange, the exchange of meanings takes place in highly structured settings, in which not all participants have the same position, the same rights, the same meanings, and not all meanings are valued equally. Perhaps one analogy might be that of a market. Culture would be that aspect of the market that referred to the kinds of commodities brought to the market, and to their modes of production. Communication would be the aspect that referred to the trade in those commodities, and the conditions under which they are traded.

The distinction reflects the social and cultural need to have two distinctly different modes of focusing on the one area. So the increasing concern with 'communication' is itself a reflection of a cultural tendency, namely the fact that western technological societies have moved into an era where information has become the major economic commodity. With the shift of emphasis from the production of material goods to the production of information comes, necessarily, a concern for the study of the processes and structures of distribution of that information. The shift from the industrial to the post-industrial period is accompanied by the need for a better understanding of communication.

Studies of communication focus on the manner in which cultural meanings are organised, on the structures within which meanings are produced, on the producers, and on the processes of the production of meaning. They give equal attention to the structures within which meanings are consumed, on the consumers, and on the processes of consumption of meaning. Above all, studies of communication and culture insist on seeing the totality of the structures, of the whole system, of the interconnectedness of all the processes.

When looked at through the focus of communication, all cultural activities take on the appearance of codes. In an important sense cultural systems such as food, furniture and clothing have some of the characteristics of language. Take food for example. Within one cultural group there is a set of items that count as possible kinds of food. Such sets tend to be characteristic of particular groups. For instance, there is an initial decision whether to regard animals as potential sources of food (the distinction between vegetarian and non-vegetarian groups); then which animals (whether foxes, dogs, cats, pigs, cows, goats, or horses; whether grubs, slugs, snails); then which parts of animals (whether all parts, or some, and which); then how these parts are to be used — whether highly processed or not (as sausage or roast). These items can be thought of as the basic units of the food-code — equivalent perhaps to words. In cooking they are combined with other 'words' (vegetables, spices, grains, fruits) to form more complex units, dishes — perhaps equivalent to sentences. In making these dishes/sentences there are rules of grammar: how to combine the meat with the spices, in what sequence, in what quantity, whether to fry, braise, grill, boil — the processes equivalent perhaps to verbs. In a meal a number of dishes are combined, again according to strict and culturally specific rules, to form the whole — a little bit like a complete text in language. And just as there are rules in language that stipulate what can be said where, by whom and to whom, when, and in what order, so there are strict rules in relation to food that specify what can count as a morning meal or an evening meal (which are themselves, of course, culturally determined). While a continental breakfast might be becoming acceptable in Australia as one kind of morning meal, it probably would not be accepted (other than in extraordinary circumstances) as an evening meal. Conversely, a seafood cocktail followed by a game casserole and a Bombe Alaska would not often appear on breakfast menus in Australia.

A very little reflection will show how other cultural systems are also organised in the form of codes, and perhaps somewhat metaphorically speaking, as 'languages'. The whole of culture is already oriented towards communication. Another point following from this is that cultural behaviour is highly constrained by a finely articulated set of rules, most of which never appear in explicit, overt form — though we quickly become aware of them if we break them by accident or by design. Some of these rules do appear: a whole industry is built on the anxieties generated through a fear of breaking the rules. Magazines such as *Vogue Living*, *Australian Gourmet*, *Home Beautiful*, *House and Garden* are, at one level, instruction manuals on how to understand and observe the rule systems of particular cultural groups.

Given that cultural behaviour is so highly articulated and rule governed, the place for individual expression is severely circumscribed. More than that, individuals grow into a culture that is already fully established, has complex sets of values and classifications, sets of rules, prohibitions and permissions. To the individual these codes appear usual, normal, natural; and s/he accepts them as the way the world is, as the proper picture of human nature, and as all that there can be. Having mastered the complexities of the culture, life is then conducted in the grooves provided by that culture. That is both a benefit in oiling the wheels of communication and a problem in providing the grooves in which it is to run.

Ways of Thinking About Communication and Culture

From what I have been saying so far you will see that it is impossible to think about communication without thinking about cultural contexts and meanings. I will sketch a model of the processes of communication by starting with the traditional model of communication, the S → M → R model, and by progressively providing a critique of that model.

As it stands, the model says that in any one communicative event there is a sender (S) who sends a message (M) to a receiver (R). We need to include the arrows in the description of the model and say that they represent two things: one, the code (C), which is used by the sender and understood by the receiver and is a shared, common code; and two, the direction of the flow of communication, from sender to receiver. This seems an entirely plausible model. But note some aspects of this model. First, it goes in one direction only, from S to R. S is the source, and R is, as it were, the target; and this makes the activities of S and R very different. S constructs the message and sends it. S is active, both in making the meaning and in transmitting it. R, however, is merely passive, receiving the message and absorbing it. So S and R are differently positioned by this model. S is active and has power; R is passive and has relatively less power. Second, the model treats S and R as asocial, isolated individuals. Nothing is said either about the context in which they are located at the time of their communication, or about the wider social positioning and place of S and R. For instance, it makes a difference whether S and R are in a conversation in their mutual home (say a husband and wife, or children), or in an argument in R's house, or in an interview in S's office, or perhaps whether R is in a lecture given by S. Furthermore, it makes a great difference whether S and R belong to the same social class, are of the same age, or of the same gender. So even if the immediate context is the same for two instances of communication, say an interview in S's office, it makes a difference whether S is an upper-class male professional talking to a lower-class female client, or whether two male legal professionals (say a barrister and a solicitor) are involved.

A third point, which needs much closer attention, is the message (M). In the S → M → R model it originates with S, who expresses a meaning that is his/her meaning, a meaning that comes from and belongs to S. But my earlier discussion has, I hope, shown that the meanings we 'have' come from the culture in which we are located. We are formed by cultural meanings and we are transmitters of culturally given meanings, rather than being expressers of 'our own' meanings. The message may in fact be a meaning of which R is already aware, which R already 'has'. Think of the many messages that are entirely determined by the culture of which we are members, so much so that they seem from one point of view quite meaningless. These are messages such as: 'Hot day, isn't it', 'Oh, I don't know, yesterday seemed much worse, today we've got a bit of a breeze at least', 'We could do with a bit of rain, though', 'We sure could' . . . This may seem a particularly trivial example, and perhaps it is; but I believe it is ubiquitous in social life. Even when the barrister and the solicitor are in conference a lot of their talk is of this kind, though of course it has a different content, a content appropriate to their professional context. The function of such messages is that of a kind of social cement, what the anthropologist Bronislaw Malinowski called 'phatic communion'.

There is nothing unidirectional about such talk; the cementing is being done by both participants equally. We should therefore at the very least remove the arrows from the model and replace them by simple lines, to indicate that both S and R already have these meanings, and that there is a mutuality about this act of communication. Perhaps if we wanted arrows, we should have them coming from that somewhat nebulous entity called culture in which S and R are located and which provides the meanings and the messages already made for both of them.

But there are many situations where the message is one R does not already have, which may be foreign to R, or where it may contradict a meaning/message that R has. S might start a conversation in the kind of way I suggested above and then move to 'And what do you think of the state of the economy? Isn't it just shocking what is happening to the dollar?' 'Yeah, it's quite worrying and the government doesn't seem to have a clue where it's going', 'Yeah, I blame the bloody unions myself, too much power by far, they're just running the bloody country into the ground', 'Well, I don't know, seems to me that the unions and the workers have done their share, profits have never been higher, the workers have got to make all the sacrifices' . . . Here R is far from passive, and does not merely passively absorb S's meaning, but reconstructs it in his or her terms. Nor is mutuality the characteristic mode here, unlike in my earlier example. This seems to me an entirely usual situation, one we would predict from our knowledge of the cultural and social diversity of society. That often leads to a situation where S and R have quite different social and cultural experiences, positions, and consequently, meanings.

The constraints I have described so far, constraints both on the mess-

age and on the senders and receivers, derive from the structures and contents of the codes in which cultural objects and meanings are organised.
The message and the code in which it is framed always have that
relationship: the nature of the code itself presents possibilities and constraints on the form and content of a message. Take the relatively simple
example of clothing. What I wear says much about who I am, who I think
I am, and how I want others to think about who I am. I can dress in a
number of different ways, each with their particular meanings. The
possibilities are given by the code of dress, organised by fashion. The
constraints are set by what I can afford to pay, by the weather, by a
decision to conform or to outrage. I can even dress 'ungrammatically' by
wearing items of clothing that belong to different styles of dress: I could
wear a dinner jacket with a pair of tennis shorts, no shirt, and thongs.
And yet, both by dressing according to a code and by dressing in contra-
vention of a code I am constrained by the code. The kinds of items of
clothing available at any one time in any one culture, even when I combine them in 'impermissible' or 'creative' ways, still constitute the limits
of what I can construct by way of a message.

Clothing is a relatively simple code by comparison with the most
highly developed and most finely nuanced cultural code, language. The
language of a particular culture is the storehouse of meanings available
to that culture. Like any storehouse it contains things from the past as
well as things that have just come into use. It contains, above all, things
in present use but which have a long history, during the course of which
they had slightly different uses and slightly different meanings. A
language is therefore not only the inventory of present meanings, but a
record, imperfectly preserved, of the past meanings of a culture. Clearly,
a code of this kind has profound effects on messages constructed in that
code. Any utterance bears the meanings of the present and the meanings
of a past that stretches from the moment just passed into an increasingly
grey and obscure past, often reaching back for thousands of years.

Quite clearly, the simple S → M → R model cannot be sustained in
that form. Receivers and senders have to be seen as socially formed per
sons, speaking the meanings of their cultural and social groups, at times
in harmony, often in discord and contention. Receivers actively reconstruct the meaning/messages they are offered — even when there may be
little or no overt sign of such activity. Senders do not send messages that
express meanings of individual origin, but meanings of social and cultural origin.

The exchange between senders and receivers is an active encounter in
which participants frequently occupy positions of unequal power. This is

so even though all receivers are active participants, and are actively engaged in the (re) construction of messages and meanings. A schoolchild in a classroom cannot resist the meanings of the teacher without encountering serious penalties, such as failure in the education system. An applicant in a job interview does not have the same power, the same range of possibilities of action as those who are interviewing her/him; even less so if the applicant needs the job. There is a need to attend closely to the social setting in which communication takes place. That will give us important information both about meanings and about the possibilities for constructing and reconstructing messages. The market in meanings is not a free market. Not all members of a society have access to all meanings; rather, meanings are distributed, available and accessible along the lines of the potent structuring principles of a society: class, gender, age, ethnicity, profession.

The picture of the communication process I have developed so far is one in which both sender and receiver are socially and culturally formed. S and R may have broadly similar cultural and social experiences and histories and present positions, and they may have entirely differing histories and positions. Both S and R are active participants in the process which is certainly not undirectional, from S to R. Rather, we might think of arrows going from S to M and from R to M, $S \rightarrow M \leftarrow R$, to indicate that there is a contestation around the meaning of the message.

More generally, we might say that the model itself has no directionality. Rather, the directionality lies in each encounter in communication. From a particular social situation and from the power differences in play in that situation we can make relatively reliable predictions about the direction the flow of communication will take. And the possibilities range very wide indeed. The extremes of this model are situations where someone is completely excluded from being a sender. Children who were supposed 'to be seen and not heard' are one instance of extremes of power that can function to silence all those who have little or no power at all in particular situations. In other situations one of the two participants may with difficulty be a sender: think, for example, of the problems of countering the messages of the mass media as a simple viewer, reader, listener. There are now largely token occasions that allow consumers of the mass media to become S: phone-in and talk-back radio, columns of readers' letters, audience participation programs on television. But there are also many occasions when R is powerful. Think of the medical practitioner listening to a nervous and inarticulate patient talking about his/her 'condition'. In this situation the doctor has complete power to reconstruct the message sent by S, and, what is more, to make the reconstruction of that message stick. It is the doctor's diagnosis both of the patient's verbal and non-verbal message and of the patient's body — treated as a text that is read for symptoms — which leads to the treatment prescribed for the patient.

So, directionality cannot be assigned to the model as such, but rather comes about in particular encounters, and is determined by the relative distribution of power in a given situation. The communication model, therefore, should be seen more as a contestation over control of the message. The message itself is a cultural construct. On the one hand it is mediated through S and her/his cultural and social position, and constrained and affected by the possibilities of meaning inherent in the code. On the other hand it is reconstructed by R in line with her/his social and cultural experience and position, and her/his orientation towards the code in which the message is framed.

To conclude this section I will briefly make some further comments on the production of the message. Our culture is one which places enormously high value on the individual and actions of the individual. This leads to a great focus on the individual creator of messages: whether as painter, sculptor, author, film-maker, composer, sportsman or woman. The force of our cultural values is to exalt individual creativity, originality and the individual genius. In my view this is an ideologically and politically motivated construct, a skewing of the reality of our social lives. All texts are social and cultural in their origin; they draw on the existing codes in a culture that always pre-exist any one text, and they draw on, borrow from, assimilate, transform other existent texts. As an (highly simplified) instance take the processes involved in making a film. Someone might have an idea, or perhaps a completed text such as a novel. This is developed by a writer skilled in producing film scripts, probably with several rewritings. The writer of the film script is not usually the same person as the writer of the initial text. The script becomes the basis for the shooting of the film. The director works on the script, in implementing it in actual locations and scenes. Before and during this process there may have been further modifications of the script due to financial problems, difficulties with the cast, clashes between novelist, scriptwriter, director, actors. During the shooting of the film the actors do their own 'rewriting' in the actual performance of the parts, and the cameramen obtain their effect through filming, lighting, and so on. The film that is shot is then edited and given a soundtrack, which adds quite specific meanings to the total. Frequently a composer is engaged to write a musical score for the film, which makes a fundamental contribution to the meaning of the film. The final product, the finished text, might be called another great film by Fellini, or Fassbender, or Spielberg, who is hailed as the originating and creative genius — though it is clear that the film has an enormously complex and multiple authorship. Very many different, sometimes contradictory, voices are present in the film, all with their own social and cultural origin. The claim of the single originating genius and author is a myth; and although it is a pervasive myth with strong motivations, a myth nevertheless. Every text has such a multiple authorship — not directly in the way the film can be shown to have, but a complex, multiple authorship nevertheless. Every sentence I write draws on many sentences I've heard or read before. Every argument I make borrows from countless other arguments. Every text I complete is cast in a form that already exists: as an essay, a chapter in a book, an introduction, an office memo, a report, a letter to the editor, a lecture, a conversation, an interview, and so on. Every text is composed of a multiplicity of culturally determined voices, drawing on other texts, in dialogue with other arguments, or with the objections of my imagined readers.

The treasured notion of the creative individual as the originator of meanings, so potent in western societies, is a myth — which functions to obscure the effects of social relations and cultural organisations for members of a society. By that device the powerless can be held responsible for their lack of power: if we're all just individuals like one another, we only have ourselves to blame for our lack of effectiveness or success. But by that device the powerful are also protected from challenge: their power is due to their individual capability, rather than to socially derived power and their cultural positioning. The myth is a powerfully conservative device that serves to maintain the way things are. For after all, if what we are and what we do and produce is due simply to ourselves, there cannot be any possibility of change, because you cannot change human nature.

The traditional S → M → R model is therefore not merely overly simplistic, it can be seen to have specific social and political meanings and implications, in that it provides a description that presents the picture in a particular way. But that, of course, is the condition of all models, all theories, my own no less than others.

One advantage the model I am sketching here has over the traditional model is that it permits us to account for all communicative encounters. Whether it is an encounter between a mass-media institution and an individual television viewer, or communication between a government department and a transnational company, or two neighbours chatting over the back fence, the one theory or model is sufficient to enable us to describe what is happening. The reason is that all meanings. whether those of the individual or those of a large organisation, are all seen as complex and as originating in particular cultural and social settings. There is therefore no need for one theory to deal with mass communication, another with interpersonal communication, and yet others with organisational communication, intercultural communication, and so on. This allows us to give one coherent account for the whole field of communication, from the largest to the smallest level.

Further Reading

Chambers, Iain *Popular Culture. The Metropolitan Experience* Methuen 1986
Corner, John and Jeremy Hawthorn *eds Communication Studies. An Introductory Reader* Edward Arnold 1985
Fiske, John *Introduction to Communication Studies* Methuen 1982
Hall, S. et al (eds) *Culture Media Language* Hutchinson 1980
Hebdige, D. *Subculture: The Meaning of Style* Methuen 1979
Sullivan, Tim *et al Key Concepts in Communication* Fontana 1984
Williams, Raymond *Keywords* Fontana 1976
———— *Culture* Fontana 1981

CHAPTER TWO

◣

Australian Society

by
Ann Curthoys

A fundamental point implicit in the view on communication put forward in this book is that communication is everywhere and always a cultural and social matter. This goes beyond the common assumption that in thinking about processes of communication 'we have to bear the (social) context in mind'. In that view there is communication on the one side, and the external, extraneous context somewhere 'out there' on the other side. The view put forward here is that such a dichotomy is wrong and fundamentally misleading. Processes of communication are social and cultural processes; social and cultural practices are always about communication.

If anything, and this may seem paradoxical and wrongheaded in a book on communication, social structures and cultural values and organisation have to be seen as primary — or rather, communication needs to be seen as primarily a social/cultural practice. Consequently, without an understanding of social structure, there can be no real understanding of communication, for communication is structured by the institutions of class, family, the organisations of the State and, in the case of most western societies, by the all-pervasive organisations of the capitalist industrialised economy. It is everywhere formed and informed by the valuations attached to gender, race, class. It is everywhere formed and affected by inequalities of power produced by these structures and values.

In putting forward such an approach, the writers of this book challenge a pervasive view of communication, which is that communication is 'just about individuals interacting'. Underlying this commonsense view is the notion that 'we are all just individuals, doing our own thing'; that when we communicate we express some inner meaning that springs from ourselves, and that when we express these meanings we do so freely, unfettered by external factors. This commonsense view is easily challenged — for instance, do you talk to your boss or teacher in the same way as you talk to your neighbour, or your lover, or to the taxman in a desk audit? And yet the view quickly re-emerges, because we are so familiar with the social and cultural forms of our society that they have become natural to us, as a 'second nature'. And in becoming part of nature they have become the way things are, and with that, invisible.

This chapter brings to our attention some of those basic aspects of social structure that are everywhere imbricated in all aspects of communication. In the first section of this chapter, several crucial concepts are described: class, the state, gender, family and kinship, capitalism and industrialisation, and relations of work in such a society. They provide the outlines of the framework of social structuring, distributions of power, and important meanings, which we need to bear in mind at all times in any serious considerations of communication. The second section of this chapter then turns to look at how these factors have come together in the history and present form of a particular society, namely Australia. This section provides an essential insight into the meanings, the cultural values, which we as members of this society share, contest, argue and struggle over; and it gives some indication of where these values come from, in the brief history of European settlement and colonial domination of the Aboriginal population. While the first section of the chapter gives an account of how communicative relations are structured in this society, the second section gives an indication of the fundamental issues that communication in this society is about: issues of race, the colonial legacy, wealth and its distribution, attitudes to the state, to politics and power generally, and the dominant myths of this society.

These are all matters of fundamental importance to any attempt at understanding communication.

Concepts in Social Theory

Capitalism and Industrialisation

The two concepts of 'industrialisation' and 'capitalism' are quite distinct, though they are often used together as in 'industrial capitalist society'. Industrialisation is a process whereby the ways in which goods and services are produced in a society are revolutionised to enable use of labour-saving technology, including the harnessing of power from water or fuel. Use of this technology historically involves the move of production from home and farm to construction site, mine, factory, and office. It also involves the growth of specialisation in production: where in pre-industrial societies most people produce most of the things they need for themselves, in industrialised societies most people work in one particular aspect of production only.

The term 'capitalism' refers to something quite different, that is, to a particular system of ownership of the property used in the production process. Capitalism derives from the term 'capital' — the stock of accumulated wealth (in the form of plant and machinery, or money to acquire them) that can be applied to the tasks of producing goods and services. In most social systems there is some form of accumulated wealth; this becomes capital only when it is applied to the task of production.

Now let us assume that this capital has been accumulated privately, as indeed it frequently was in the early phases of historical capitalism. Through a whole series of historical events, a class of people has emerged which owns capital, and another which does not. The latter group also does not own land, or owns so little that it cannot survive on it. Its members cannot produce their own food, clothing, shelter and other goods, and must work for the owners of capital to earn wages which will enable them to buy the necessaries of life.

As capitalism develops historically, this arrangement, called a wage-relation, enters into ever-increasing spheres of human activity. But it does not enter all of them, and not everyone is bound into it. Children, for example, do not work for wages (though in the early phases of capitalism many of them did). Housework and childcare are still often done privately in the home and the people who do it gain their support not directly in the form of wages for work done, but indirectly, generally through wages for other work done either by the childcarer or by other members of the household, or perhaps in the form of a charity or welfare payment.

Capitalism, then, is a system where the owners of capital employ the non-owners. Although it can exist without and before industrialisation, in the modern world capitalist societies are industrial, or at least industrialising, societies, for accumulation of capital on a large scale depends on the acquisition of efficient — industrial — methods of production.

Modern social theory tends to divide according to which of these two processes is seen as the key feature of modern society. On the one hand, there are those social theories that focus on the characteristics of industrial society — scale, complexity, bureaucracy, the decline of kinship as an organising principle in social relations, and centralisation of political authority. A classic example of this school is Emile Durkheim, a French sociologist who was concerned with questions of social cohesion and the difference industrialisation makes to the ways that social cohesion is maintained. On the other hand, there are those social theories that focus on the characteristics of capitalist society — the private ownership of property, the wage-relation, and the ways inequalities in wealth and power arise not accidentally but structurally from the very nature of capitalism itself. A classic example of this school is Karl Marx, a German theorist who attempted to define how and why capitalism emerged, and how and why it would end. Somewhere between those two lies Max Weber, another German theorist, writing in the early twentieth century, who was concerned with both. We'll encounter all three theorists again as this chapter proceeds.

Capitalism is characterised by a high level of mobility as both labour and capital move with and across national political boundaries, to meet each other. The large-scale export of capital, in the form of investment, and the large-scale export of people, in the form of migration as people seek more economic opportunities than they can find at home, have been ordering features of capitalism for several centuries. This migration, inhibited though it has been by all sorts of political, cultural, social and geographic factors, has seen the transformation of the ethnic composition of entire continents, particularly Australia and America.

To 'mobility', then, we must add 'expansionism' as a characteristic of capitalism. This expansion of capital, trading relationships and people into the previously non-capitalist world was often initiated and managed by the strong national governments that had emerged either before or along with the growth of capitalist forms of economic relationships.

These new nation-states were able to exert considerable power over populations outside their own territorial borders. They financed and organised much of the exploration of the non-capitalist world, as materials were sought for the new industries. They financed and organised the conquest of territories needed to secure those raw materials. They established in the non-capitalist world a multitude of colonies, for economic and strategic reasons. One of the main, if not *the* main, resources used in these colonies were the local populations, who could be forced or persuaded to become labour for the processes of producing food, or extracting raw materials for industrial production. For this whole process to occur, these capitalist states had not only to set up administrative mechanisms in the newly acquired territories, but also to preside over the appropriation of land. In the process, the indigenous populations were either displaced and even exterminated, or drawn into production for a world market.

Capitalism has been characterised not only by its mobility and its expansionism, but also by the cyclical nature of its development. In periods of boom, the level of capital accumulation is high, there is little unemployment, and productivity increases. In periods of depression, the owners of capital cannot find sufficient markets for their products, and so many enterprises contract or collapse and unemployment soars. These cycles generally affect the world capitalist system as a whole, since the different national economies are closely interlinked through investment, trade, transnational companies, and financial exchanges.

The Organisation of Work under Industrial Capitalism

There are many who argue, following the American writer Harry Braverman, that there is a long-run tendency under industrial capitalism for employers to increase their control of the way work is done, and for workers to lose theirs. Increasingly they had to work with new machines with which they were unfamiliar. Whole new industries developed where there was little worker tradition about how work ought to be done. The task of co-ordinating all these workers, setting them to work on the new machines, and enforcing discipline about hours and speed of work was taken up by the new owners of the means of production, the capitalists, or employers.

During the nineteenth century in the industrialising countries greater knowledge of management techniques was developed. Especially with the success of trade union and other pressures for the limitation of the working day (from 16 hours to 12, and then to 10 by the 1860s) it became essential to know how to get the maximum value out of the remaining 10 hours in the working day. The breakthrough came with the work and ideas of the American Frederick Winslow Taylor. His ideas have since become known as Taylorism, or scientific management, and their effect on management techniques is still felt today. The story of Taylor's experiments with management is told in detail in Harry Braverman's *Labor and Monopoly Capital.*

The essence of his approach was that management had increasingly to gather knowledge of work skills to itself, to develop rules and routines and system of work which it could then require the workers to follow. As industrial plants became larger and more complex, the need to study the whole work process increased, and only *management* could afford the time to conduct such a study, to bring together an understanding of how the whole plant, or factory, ought to operate. Workers would be confined to specialised tasks, so that they became less skilled, able to claim only low pay, and unable to challenge management's authority in any serious way.

Braverman's theory, first published in 1974, aroused great interest in the study of work. The main criticism has come from those who argue that workers in trade unions were often able to insist on the maintenance of skilled occupations with higher rates of pay, despite management's attempts to break the work down into several low-skill components. The question of retaining skill in work — and the pay and relative autonomy that skill brings with it — has been seen as a battleground, where neither management nor workers has been wholly victorious.

Class

One of the most important characteristics of industrial capitalism is the creation of social classes. This is not peculiar to capitalism; other kinds of societies, for example feudal society, produce social classes too. But the classes that emerge in industrial-capitalist society are of a specific kind. Just how we understand class in modern society is a central, and very controversial, problem for social theory. The debates on class are usually based on a denial or an affirmation of the view of class put forward by Karl Marx and Frederick Engels in the mid-nineteenth century. To understand class we need to trace these debates.

In the *Manifesto of the Communist Party,* Marx and Engels put forward the view that all societies are divided into antagonistic classes — master/slave, lord/serf, bourgeoisie/proletariat. Under industrial capitalism, they said, these class relationships were becoming increasingly simple and increasingly hostile — the rich were getting richer and fewer, the poor were getting poorer and more numerous. This economic polarisation was increasingly giving rise to a political polarisation, so that both capitalists and workers became better organised. Being far more numerous, the workers, once they were organised, would win the battle and establish some new, presumably classless, kind of society. So the view of the *Manifesto* is one of inevitable conflict, escalating to the point where an entire social system would be overthrown and a new one created.

But Marx's views on class were not confined to those expressed in the *Manifesto*. While he continued to believe that polarisation would intensify as capitalism developed, he also recognised that the class structure of mid-nineteenth century Western Europe was a good deal more complicated. He noted the division within the bourgeoisie and the proletariat and the evidence of the in-between groups — the self-employed and the professionals. His key concern was to see the effects of this complicated class structure on ideology and politics, and he noted how in France during the period after the 1848 revolution the balance of power kept changing as various classes formed alliances which then dissolved. The changes in control of state power, in particular, rested on the difficulty the fractured capitalist class had in maintaining its own unity.

Marx and Engels views related class very closely to economic position. That is, classes arise when a group of people has a common relationship to the means of production, for example as wage earners, self-employed, rural peasants, owners of capital, landowners. But for Marx and Engels there was a distinction between mere economic position and class, or if you like, between economic class and class generally. Class in the broader sense implied not only common economic position, but also a *consciousness* of that position. Thus a group of people without that consciousness was like 'a sack of potatoes', and Marx saw the mid-nineteenth century French peasants as in this position. They had an economic situation in common, but they did not seek their own political organisations to express their distinctive demands. A class of people with that consciousness was more properly a social class in Marx's sense. Capitalism contained within it the seeds of its own destruction because it created a working class which would necessarily develop a form of consciousness that would lead it to seek to end its economic exploitation and political subordination.

This general view of class and class consciousness has been subject to many criticisms. The most basic criticism is that instead of polarising into two main antagonistic classes, the effect of industrial capitalism has been to create a vast middle class, between the upper class on the one hand, and the working class on the other. The growth of this class has meant that even if capitalism does continually produce inequalities, an increasing proportion of people do quite well from the system. As a result, it is argued, the dissent of the nineteenth century has died down and been replaced by a political system where disagreements are in fact minor and where talk of overthrowing capitalism altogether is rare.

One of the first people to remark on this development was Max Weber. He pointed to the growth of bureaucracies — the development of a vast army of administrative, technical and clerical workers in both private business and the public services — and pointed out that this would create a large group of people who were well educated and better paid than the factory workers. Such people, he pointed out, were inclined to see their personal interests as lying within the existing social order, and so would tend to side with employers rather than factory workers. A quite similar view was advanced by Ralf Dahrendorf, in a book published in 1959. He, like Weber, stressed the importance of the administrative and clerical workers — the bureaucrats — and provided more recent empirical data to back up this view. Theorists like Dahrendorf and many others only had to point to the statistics that — depending on how you classified various occupations — showed that the white-collar sections of the workforce could range from 30 per cent in Britain to 50 per cent in the U.S.A. Whichever way you looked at it, the white-collar occupations had grown enormously since 1848, and made Marx and Engels predictions of polarisation seem rather questionable.

Marxists have considerable trouble trying to respond to these criticisms. Some agreed that there has indeed been a rapid growth in the size of the 'middle class', and have attempted to develop explanations for this in terms of the changing requirements of capitalism. Others have argued that while there is indeed a large group of better-off workers, with higher levels of education and pay, its members are still essentially working class, having no resources for survival other than their own skills and capacity to work.

The second main line of criticism of the view of class put in the *Manifesto* has centred around the problem of the upper, or ruling class. Whereas once the owners of a business or company ran or managed that company, increasingly the functions of ownership and management were becoming separated. Ownership, it is argued, was becoming more diffuse, especially with the growth of public companies and corporations in which capital was raised by floating shares on the open market. Instead of one or two owners of capital, you now had thousands of owners of shares who exerted little or no control over the way the company in which they held shares was run. This control passed away from the owners to professional managers, people who might not own any shares at all, but who were experts in business or company management. Thus ownership did not confer the control and power it had in the nineteenth century, and power and wealth were not so automatically linked.

There have been several responses to this rise of a distinct managerial group. One has been to say that these managers are part of the growing new middle class, another to see them as a distinct part of the capitalist or ruling class, and yet another to point out the fact that most managers do in fact own shares and so the distinction between owners and managers is more apparent than real. A fourth view has been to argue that not all managers are the same: some are the heads of large corporations, wielding immense economic power, and are unquestionably members of the ruling or upper class; others work for quite small businesses and — although on a higher salary than most workers — are in the same position as those workers ultimately in that they can be hired and fired at will, and are answerable to higher management and to a definable company owner.

A third criticism of the view of class advanced in the *Manifesto* has been a questioning of its view of the working class becoming inevitably more organised and united in opposition to the bourgeoise. The working class, it is argued, is increasingly differentiated and divided amongst itself, and is therefore unable to unite to overthrow the capitalists. Ralf Dahrendorf again is an important exponent of this view, pointing to the ways different degrees of skill divide the working class into skilled, semi-skilled and unskilled categories. Thus not only is the capitalist class divided into owners and managers, but the working class also is divided, with trade unions protecting only certain sections of the working class rather than the working class as a whole.

More recently, in the 1970s, a great deal of attention has been given to the ways the working class is divided within itself and so does not achieve very great political unity beyond, perhaps, a majority support for labour or social democratic parties. There are seen to be four basic sources of division. First there are differences in access to 'good' jobs and 'bad' ones, that is, differences between those involving skill, reasonable levels of pay and reasonable job security and those which entail little skill, low pay and no job security. Second, there are differences between indigenous and immigrant workers, between workers of different ethnic groups. Recent research in Europe, the USA and Australia indicates that immigrant and minority group workers will tend to get the worst jobs, and so will have little in common with the better paid, more secure and often more skilled indigenous workers of those countries. Third, there is hostility between the employed and the unemployed, which grows as unemployment rises. The income differential between the unemployed and the employed is very considerable and the less temporary the condition of being unemployed becomes, the greater the division between the two groups. Fourth, there are differences based on gender. Not only do migrants and indigenous workers tend to fill different parts of the job market, but women also tend to enter jobs of lower skill and pay and higher labour turnover than those entered by men.

This last source of division highlights a very important issue for class analysis in general. I have already referred to this briefly: it is that classes are composed not only of owners of capital, or self-employed, or wage earners, but also of people dependent on those owners and earners, or on private charity or the state. Apart from unemployment, the most common sources of dependence are based on age and gender.

Gender

Gender is a profoundly important organising principle in social life, no less in industrial capitalist societies than in other or earlier ones. A social distinction between 'men' and 'women' is common to all societies. This distinction is based, in the first instance, on biological difference, more specifically the biological duality in human reproduction. Both men and women are needed (still) for the process of human reproduction, but only women (still) can give birth. Yet in all known societies the categories 'male' and 'female' have a significance which goes far beyond this biological difference.

Much theoretical energy has been devoted to trying to determine what is common across very different social systems and historical periods in this social construction of male and female. What is it, if anything, that is always present? Male domination and female subordination? A sexual division of labour? Male control over women's bodies? The high social evaluation of the male over the female? The exertion of male control through greater physical strength? The construction through the family of gendered identities? Notions about the essential (and proper) nature of women and men?

Only two of the above would I be confident of: a sexual division of labour (though this is not *necessarily* universal, only observably so), and the construction of gendered identities. For the others, I would rather set aside the task of determining whether they are universal, and confine this discussion to the observable patterns in modern industrial capitalism, especially in Australia.

First, the sexual division of labour. I mentioned earlier that under industrial capitalism, not all human activities are drawn entirely into the market, into the wage-relation characteristic of capitalism. In particular, childcare and domestic labour have been only partially drawn in. This does not affect men and women indiscriminately or equally. Women's association with childcare and household tasks is far closer than that of men. This arises in the first instance from the biological facts of birth and lactation, that a woman's relationship to a child is more primary and indisputable than that of a man. It arises in the second instance from the social conviction that women *ought* to have the immediate care of children. In fact, of course, once babies can survive without breast-feeding, it is quite possible for children to be cared for entirely by men. But this rarely happens, for the close biological relationship between mother and child has laid a basis for the belief that children are more appropriately nurtured by women. This conviction is shared by women and men, whether they belong to the class of owners or non-owners of capital, and can be called the 'ideology of motherhood'.

In societies where there is no wage-relation, and where life is sustained through hunting and gathering or through pastoral and/or cottage production, a differentiation in men's and women's tasks will be evident. Generally, both will contribute to production, and women's tasks will include, but not be confined to, the care of young children. Food, shelter, clothing and other necessities are shared within the household or family group. Both men and women depend on the work performed by the other.

When a wage-relation has been established, new issues arise. Each household will need at least one profit maker or wage earner. (If it has neither, private charity or state support will be necessary for survival.) Very often it will have more than one. But child and household care take time, and the household must in some way find ways for that labour-time to be provided. If it cannot, the level of material comfort, hygiene and health of both adults and children will be extremely low. This is indeed what happened in many households in Britain at the height of the Industrial Revolution. For the sources of labour to be continually renewed and kept in a condition where they can be useful to capital, this labour-time must be found. It has traditionally been found via what is known as the 'family-household system'.

A household is simply a group of people living together in the same residence, sharing the same facilities. Most people in Australia today live in households, though some live in institutions, ranging from military barracks to nursing homes and prisons. Furthermore, a high percentage of households are *family* households, the remainder being single-person households (including a large number of elderly people) and households containing several unrelated people. Under family households we now include a variety of forms. One is the traditional nuclear family household of a woman, her husband and their children. Others include married couples without children, single parents with children, adult siblings sharing a household, households with a couple with children from former marriages, and households with any of these plus another relative, say a grandparent. At any one time, only 17 per cent of households in Australia today are of the traditional nuclear family type.

Family and Kinship

In much modern discussion, the term 'family' is often used to mean only the traditional co-resident family. When conservatives talk about defending and strengthening the family and feminists talk about abolishing it, both have this kind of family in mind. But there is also another common meaning of family, which is one's stock of relatives, whether they co-reside or not. These relatives are one's kin, and kinship is used to refer to the ties that exist between those who are seen as related either through birth or marriage. So kinship is concerned with the ways in which sexuality is socially organised and regulated, parentage assigned and transferred from one generation to the next. Kinship, then, relates to the ways in which human reproduction is socially understood.

In societies other than industrial capitalist ones, kinship is generally a significant organiser of social relations. In particular, the organisation of both the production and consumption of goods and services is very largely according to kinship relations. In capitalist societies, kinship loses some of its importance. The organisation of production and distribution of economic goods and services is not usually along kinship lines, though family businesses persist, and goods are indirectly distributed within the household, itself usually involving some kinship ties. But workplaces generally consist of unrelated people, and political organisations and pressure groups are not primarily kinship groups.

Even with this decline in the importance of kinship as an organising principle, the family-based household nevertheless remains important. Marriage and the family-household system involve not only emotional ties, but are also important economic institutions. There is some debate as to how and why it was that the model of male breadwinner and female full-time housewife and children was established. One line of argument is represented well by two authors, Michele Barrett and Sue Himmelweit. Both sketch out a history of the effect of industrialisation on the family-household system. They argue that in the early stages both men and women were employed as wage-labourers. This led to appalling conditions in both home and factory; middle-class reformers and male workers organised in male unions combined to force the women out of various occupations and into the home. Capitalists benefited because male workers and their children were better cared for, and male workers benefited as they were now protected from women's cheap labour in the workplace, were cared for at home, and could now receive wages high enough to support themselves, their wives and children. Women continued to work only in certain occupations, for low wages, and so were still — even if wage earners — dependent on male incomes. The reason male unionists colluded in women's confinement to a few low-pay occupations was that they believed, like their masters, that a woman's place was in the home.

Other authors, particularly Jane Humphries and Johanna Brenner and Maria Ramas, give a different account. Jane Humphries stresses that the drive to enable working-class married women to stay at home, and to keep single women out of male occupations, was not imposed on working-class women by working-class men, but was, rather, jointly fought for by both women *and* men, for both perceived it as a necessary strategy for survival under the harsh conditions of nineteenth century industrial capitalism. Brenner and Ramas emphasise that the key influence on the emergence of a male-breadwinner/female-non-earning-childcare system was not sexist ideology but the incompatibility of childcaring with industrial forms of work. Although it was true that male workers believed a woman's place was in the home, the tenuousness of women's place in the workforce arose less from this belief than from the continuing need to care for children outside the industrial workplace. The biological facts of childbirth and lactation made it more logical for women than men to play this caring role.

At issue here is the question of how much relative importance do we give ideology and biology in explaining the attachment of women rather than men to childcaring. It would seem clear that both were important. What was particularly important was the increased incompatibility of childcaring and income-earning activity. The separation of the workplace from the home, and the necessity to earn wages in order to survive, together meant that women and men now had widely differing relationships to the process of production. Even so, working-class married women did not abandon wage labour altogether, working intermittently and casually to supplement their husbands' and children's income. These conditions, and their lower level of unionisation, worked together to ensure their continuing cheapness in the labour market.

During the twentieth century certain changes have emerged. First, some women have entered the more skilled occupations, and women share with men the growth in access to higher education. Second, childbearing has become a less effective brake on women's entering wage labour, partly as family size decreased, and partly with greater use of substitute childcare while mothers worked for wages. Both these developments have accelerated the demand for equal pay, which was formally gained by the 1970s, though in practice women still tend to fill the lower paid jobs in a greater proportion than men do. The ideology of motherhood persists, but is now modified to allow for a combination of motherhood and wage work. Even so, men's responsibilities for childcare have not increased substantially, and women continue to find that their opportunities for childcaring and wage work are each limited by the other.

The State

In the earlier discussion of industrial capitalism I pointed out that its rise was associated with the strengthening, both internally and externally, of European nation-states. It is time to look more closely at theories of 'the state' itself.

The state is, in brief, that constellation of institutions that govern — parliament, the public service (the bureaucracy), courts, prisons, police, the military, and secret intelligence services. A key issue for modern social theory is the degree to which the state represents the wishes and interests of all the people it governs, and the degree to which it represents the interests and wishes of particular groups or classes, or, perhaps, of no-one but itself. Once again we must look first at the views of both Marx and Weber.

Max Weber's view of the modern state rested on his understanding of it as the kind of state industrialised — rather than specifically capitalist — societies produce. Two of his major concerns were with legitimacy and bureaucracy.

In relation to the state, legitimacy refers to the capacity of the political system to maintain the general public belief that the existing political institutions in a society are good and appropriate ones. Weber agreed that all states, by definition, have a monopoly on the use of force and coercion at a public level. How they differ is not in their monopolisation of force, but in the degree to which they are seen as legitimate and hence the degree to which they need to actually exert the powers of coercion they all formally hold. A state that secures law and order only on the basis of force and coercion is one which has little legitimacy in the eyes of the members of the society. States achieve legitimacy, according to Weber, in one of three ways: first, through tradition, the idea that this is the way it has always been; second, through the exceptional personal appeal of the leader, for instance Churchill, de Gaulle, Lenin, Hitler, Castro; and last, through the notion of legality, a belief that power is wielded in a way that is legal, bound by constitutions, laws, rules, conventions. Any state might have attached to it one or other of these forms of legitimacy, or perhaps a combination of two or three — tradition, personal charisma, legality.

Weber's second main concern was with the question of state bureaucracy. He argued that industrialisation brought with it a particular kind of state bureaucracy. The growth in the size and complexity of the tasks of public administration was so great that the state bureaucrats, or public servants, could no longer be effectively controlled by politicians or by parliament. The state bureaucrats, he said, tend to link with big business, and their tasks become so technical and complex that politicians cannot understand what the bureaucrats are doing and can do little to control their actions. Because his main concern was with the political problems industrialisation produces, and his analysis of those problems was meant to apply to all industrialised societies, whether capitalist or state socialist, Weber has been seen to be useful for an analysis of the state bureaucracies in the Soviet Union and Eastern Europe.

By contrast, Marx's concern was with the capitalist state specifically. He regarded it as the political means whereby the political needs of the economically powerful classes were met. These classes became ruling classes by virtue of their economic power and their effective domination of the state and its agencies. While the state guaranteed its power through its monopoly of force, the ruling classes guaranteed theirs through their domination of the state itself.

The Marxist theory of the state was developed by Lenin in the context of the Russian Revolution. Lenin, like Weber, saw parliament under liberal democracies as essentially a talking shop, a screen for the real decision making by the bureaucracy. But whereas Weber saw this as a problem to be overcome, Lenin said it couldn't be overcome since the real purpose of parliament was not to rule, only to legitimate the realities of class domination. The problem, then, was class domination itself; only when there were no classes could the state cease to function as the organ of class rule. Working-class parties, such as labour or socialist parties, could never control the state by virtue of a victory in parliament. The bureaucracy, the military and the police would continue to be interlinked with the economically dominant class, so that the working class party in government would either succumb and resort to maintaining class domination or be forced out of office.

The third main way of approaching the state has been the pluralist view. This is represented by a wide variety of political scientists, notably Robert A. Dahl. Pluralists argue that in western democracies parliament is the place where different political forces, pressure and interests are registered. As the balance of forces in a society alters, so the elected representatives in parliament will change in response to the shifting winds of opinion. Even when there are elites within different power structures, in business, in the trade unions, or in political parties, no single elite can dominate. The role of parliament and therefore the state as a whole is to accommodate and reconcile them all; it is a mirror of society. This view emphasises the plurality in modern industrial society itself, and the role of political pressure groups as expressions of that social plurality. The end result is that while some people are more powerful than others, no-one has a monopoly on power and no-one is entirely without it.

A key difference between the pluralists and both Marx and Weber is that the former assume that parliament does indeed control all aspects of the state, and that the people control parliament. Both Marx and Weber look to the power of the non-elected aspects of the state — the police, military, secret intelligence, courts, civil service, — and to the very imperfect control that any one parliament has over them. Furthermore, pluralists rarely point out how much pressure groups are dependent for their influence not only on the size of their membership (their popularity), but also on the economic resources they can command. In this way pressure groups reflect not only competing political views, but also broad economic groupings and interests.

These debates take on a special importance in arguments over what is generally called the welfare state. This has arisen in the nineteenth and especially the twentieth century, to fill the gap left between the economic support required by the total population and the support actually received from owners of capital in the form of wages. Some of this gap has always been filled by private charity, but increasingly the state has intervened, providing institutions, services, and cash payments to sustain the part of the population that has insufficient or no access to the wages necessary to buy the means of survival. This role arises because states exist to maintain political stability, which has come in part to rest on a sustaining of the impoverished groups in the population. Such groups always arise, especially in the depression periods of the capitalist cycle, because industrial capitalism has entailed the loss of the means of direct subsistence (through farming and cottage production) for most of the population.

Some argue that the welfare state has arisen primarily to keep workers politically quiescent. By removing the worst effects of capitalism (e.g. starvation through unemployment), it protects capitalists from the logical consequences — worker resistance and revolution — of their profit-making activities. In reply, others view welfare provisions such as pensions and benefits as necessities (under capitalism), wrung by working-class struggle through the state. Still others point out that the effect of welfare and other benefits is not to redistribute wealth from rich to poor, capital to labour, but rather to redistribute it a little more evenly between the non-owners. Debates over taxation and welfare benefits are in effect debates over whether the state can and should play a role in wealth redistribution, and if so, what kind of redistribution.

So with this bundle of concepts — industrialisation, capitalism, colonialism, class, gender, family and kinship, the state — we can now turn to an examination of Australian history, society and politics.

Australian History and Society

The British Takeover

The process whereby the Australian continent came to be a site for industrial capitalist society was bloody, violent, and — in historical terms — short. It was a process generated by several late eighteenth century developments, including the British desire for a base in the South Pacific as an aid to certain imperial ends, and the need to find an outlet for Britain's overcrowded prisons. The decision, taken in 1786, to establish a penal colony at Botany Bay, was based on the assumption that the indigenous inhabitants — later known to the British as Aborigines — had no prior right of occupation.

The British colonisers knew little of the Aboriginal society they set out to displace, and even now our knowledge can be partial only. But we do know that its economy was based on hunting, fishing and gathering of plant foods. In order to carry out these activities people lived in small bands, consisting of between 20 and 100 related people. The work was divided according to sex, where the men were responsible for hunting, women for gathering, with fishing either shared or a male or female task depending on the group. The variation in the nature of the land and food sources was great, ranging from the desert areas in the centre of the continent, to vast grasslands and the well-watered coastal regions. In general the plant foods and small game provided by the women formed the basis of everyday diet, while the larger game caught by the men provided the more protein-rich, high-status food.

But human contact, interaction and belonging were not confined to these bands. Each person belonged also to a larger group, often called a clan, by virtue of their father's clan membership, or their mother's, or by their presumed place of conception. Because clans were exogenous, that is, you could not marry a member of your own clan, each band contained members of more than one clan. And each clan had members in a large number of bands.

Land was not 'owned' in the European sense. Clans traditionally had rights to areas of land, called estates. Bands had the right to range over a certain area of land called a range. The ranges would form part of an estate, or could overlap between two estates. Thus the ranges were important as units that could be used for food gathering, that is, for economic purposes, while the estates were significant for religious belonging.

Each person in Aboriginal society had a complex system of belonging. First there was membership of the immediate family group, then of a band, then of a clan, and finally of a tribe — a group of clans. Each of these belongings had a complex set of rules attached to it, defining how food was to be shared, how sexual relations were to be conducted, how religious observance was to be carried out, and how wrongdoing was to be punished. While age and gender were important mechanisms for conferring authority, there was no governing group as such.

On to this people and their economic and political structure was imposed another, totally different. The imposition came first through the establishment of convict settlements on the east and southern coast, principally at Sydney and Hobart. Later, free settlements were established in South Australia and Western Australia, while those that had been convict settlements became free colonies — Victoria, Queensland, New South Wales and Tasmania. The differences between Aboriginal and British colonial society were profound. Whereas Aboriginal society had been stateless, from the beginning the colonies were governed by a powerful state authority. The invasion itself was decided upon and organised by the British state, and British authority was paramount for the first seventy years of settlement. The governor was responsible not to the people of Australia, white or black, but to the British government. These governors were appointed to carry out the policies of the British government in each colony. In practice it was the British Secretary of State, responsible for all colonial affairs, not just Australia, who made most of the important decisions. The governor had the military and police forces at his disposal, and the majority of the people had few civil rights.

Yet this absolute power was gradually checked. Governors found they could not easily carry out British government directives. Powerful groups emerged to challenge governors' prerogatives, on the basis of the development of a local capitalist class. At first the small convict settlements had little that was capitalist about them in their internal economic structure. When the settlement at Sydney Cove was established, the government was the only employer. All farming, building, domestic service and other work was carried out under the agency of the state. All farms, for example, were government owned and run. But soon a class of private employers emerged. Army and navy officials and some ex-convicts took advantage of the government's practice of handing out grants of land, irrespective of whether the considerable Aboriginal resistance to the seizure of land had been defeated. A class of labourers emerged too. Convicts were formally under government control, but they were frequently assigned to work for private employers. Within a few years there had been a shift from government to private farming, and the process of accumulating private capital within the colony itself had begun.

It was the development of sheep farming especially that ensured the success of private enterprise in the new colonies. Once New South Wales was discovered to be ideal for wool growing, the ranks of the owners were swelled by well-off free immigrants, who at first also gained land grants from the government. But as the settlement spread inland and along the coasts, it was getting too large for effective government control. Wanting to limit the settlement within certain boundaries, and also to gain revenue from the sale of land, governments stopped giving land away and began to sell it, but only within the specified boundaries.

The sheep-farmers did not obey these instructions. They knew there was excellent sheep and cattle grazing land beyond the boundaries, and simply went out to the new areas with their convict servants and 'squatted' on the land. What was the government to do? In fact, it allowed the situation to continue, for two reasons: first, in the 1820s and 1830s the supply of convicts from Britain was growing rapidly, a product of social and economic distress in Britain. The squatters could employ these extra convicts. Second, these squatters were often wealthy and powerful men, whom the government could not afford to antagonise. So it accepted the movement beyond the boundaries, charged the squatters a small fee for the right to lease the land, and sent them convicts to work it.

Governors were forced to make other concessions. The wealthier colonists resisted the use of convicts and ex-convicts in the colonial administration; governors soon found they could rely on them less, and had to rely more on free immigrants and the native-born to fill the ranks of the administration. From 1824 governors were forced to take the advice of local landowners, formally represented on a Legislative Council.

Landowners, businessmen, professionals, and tradesmen all became groups that opposed the governor. In response to these pressures and the growing complexity of governing, the British authorities altered the nature of the Legislative Council in the 1840s. It was now partly appointed by the governor and partly elected by men of property, and could initiate and veto certain kinds of legislation. Furthermore, the governors during the period from the 1820s and 1840s found that they were forced to institute such practices as a jury system, an independent magistracy, and freedom of assembly and the press. Twelve thousand miles was a long distance across which to administer a colony, and it was inevitable that governing institutions would have to be developed here to administer an increasingly large and complex society.

But a substantial transfer of state power would not occur while convict transportation continued. By the 1840s the system's days were numbered. With the Australian colonies becoming economically successful, it was more sensible to encourage people to migrate freely. A land where work was plentiful and relatively better paid had ceased to be a deterrent anyway. The British government began sponsoring and financing free immigration from Britain to Australia, and the practice increased through the 1840s and 1850s. Transportation ended in the eastern colonies in the 1840s, and to Western Australia in 1869. The basis was thus laid for the transfer of state power from Britain to the colonies themselves.

Self-Government and the Persecution of the Aboriginal Population

From Britain's point of view, self-government for the colonies presented no great problems, for the new colonial governments could be relied on, for economic and cultural reasons, to follow policies advantageous to Britain. And in fact, when self-government was granted to all colonies except Western Australia in the mid 1850s, it was not full self-government, for issues of foreign policy were still subject to British scrutiny and direction. Governors were still appointed by the British monarch, though these governors now held formal rather than real power. Economically, a colonial relationship continued to exist. With manufacturing very underdeveloped, the colonies provided good markets for British manufactured goods. The colonies sent raw materials, especially wool and gold, to Britain. British capitalists also exported capital, setting up large sheep and cattle stations, and making huge loans to the colonial governments for railway development and other public works.

This entire process had brought the British settlers into conflict with the Aborigines. Early expectations of little or no resistance were not realised. Aborigines wanted to retain the use of their land in the traditional way; the British wanted the same land for the purposes of farming and commercial development. The earliest skirmishes occurred in Sydney in 1788, and continued as guerilla warfare throughout the continent, the last clash occurring as late as 1928 in the Northern Territory. In these conflicts Europeans had the advantage of superior weapons and greater numbers. Occasionally some sheep and cattle stations were abandoned because of the strength of Aboriginal resistance but the settlers could always try again, which they did. Aboriginal resistance often took the form of spearing European-introduced animals, as these were destroying the sources of native food and were known to be valued by the Europeans. At times it took the form of attacks on Europeans themselves. For their part, the European invaders responded by all-out attacks on Aboriginal groups, very often not in response to an Aboriginal attack but as a preparation for settlement of a new area. These all-out attacks came to be called, euphemistically, 'punitive expeditions', but are now referred to as massacres. Even so, despite the bloodiness and violence of this process, more Aboriginal life was lost through disease than through direct warfare. Smallpox epidemics were especially destructive, but so were respiratory and other diseases.

The gradual transfer of political rule from Britain to Australia meant very little for the Aborigines, as the new colonial governments pursued policies very similar to those of the British government. The extension of settlement continued to be guaranteed through the use of force; the techniques of the punitive expedition were continued. If anything, the situation became worse for Aborigines, as the new colonial governments were run or supported by people who had gained from their own colonial experience a fear and hatred of Aborigines during the periods of conflict, and a contempt for them once they became a defeated minority. The Native Police (a police force consisting of Aborigines from distant areas) were increasingly used as a cheap and effective means of quelling Aboriginal resistance. This was especially true of Queensland, most of which was settled after the British withdrawal.

Those who survived the massacres and diseases maintained distinct communities, combining some traditional food-getting and ways of life.

But overwhelmingly they now had to work for European employers for survival, and many were employed as cheap labour, especially on the sheep and cattle stations. Governments established policies of keeping Aborigines on specially set-aside reserves and denying them political and legal rights. This was done to keep them out of towns, to maintain a labour supply for local pastoralists, and to enable further destruction of traditional Aboriginal culture through programs of christianising and education.

The New Imperialism and 'The Commonwealth'

Subsequent economic development in Australia was affected by the changing world capitalist system. Colonialism from around 1870 entered a new phase, often referred to as the 'new imperialism', lasting until the outbreak of world war in 1914. With the growth of industrial capitalism in nations other than Britain — for example, Germany, the United States, Belgium and Italy — the desire of all these powers for secure markets, access to raw materials and investment opportunities, was intense. Almost all of Africa, a good part of Asia, and many Pacific Islands had, by the First World War, been conquered, with the military resistance of indigenous populations on the whole effectively suppressed. The territory covered by the colonial powers and their possessions now covered 85 per cent of the earth's land surface.

As industrialisation proceeded within the colonising powers, their need for food from the rest of the world was intensified. As a result, more and more of the world was drawn upon as primary producers for the industrialised nations. Previously self-contained economic regions were drawn into a world economy, involving an international division of labour whereby the leading industrial nations made and sold manufactured products and the rest of the world supplied them with raw materials and food.

Australia was part of this world system, this international division of labour. From the 1850s to the 1890s the Australian colonies experienced a long period of economic boom, based on the export of primary products. This came to an abrupt end in 1890-91, as the colonies felt the shockwaves from the economic depression in Britain. Banks collapsed, the price of wool fell drastically, the rest of the economy was affected, and unemployment soared. Although the economy began to expand again by the turn of the century, some argue that the Australian economy did not fully recover before an even greater depression hit in the 1930s.

Important political changes flowed during this period from the transfer of state power from Britain to the colonies themselves in the 1850s

(1890 in Western Australia). Some were in the area of democratic rights. The first parliament in each colony quickly passed legislation for universal male suffrage. In the early 1890s the principle of 'one man one vote' became law, and between 1894 and 1908 voting rights were extended to women in colony after colony. Others were to do with the structure of politics. Political parties were slow to emerge, especially in New South Wales. Until the 1890s parliamentary members were elected as independents — there were no parties as such. These independent members joined loose combinations within parliament, organised around a leader. This system relied on the fact that the political differences between members were not very great. By the late 1880s, differences in views began to harden, and parties began to form. In particular, the growing trade union movement sought to influence government decisions not only through pressure brought from outside, but also through getting elected people they could trust. Through the 1890s, a labour party (later adopted as the Australian Labor Party) was gradually formed in each colony, and elected members of parliament to press for distinctive pro-labour policy. At times these Labor MPs held the balance of power. The non-Labor groupings also began to organise themselves more strongly.

It is around the turn of the century that we can see our modern political structure emerging. Not only did recognisable political parties take shape, but also colonial governments were transformed from independent political units with direct ties to Britain to members, as state governments, of a Federal system. For a host of reasons, not least of which was the need for economic co-ordination across colonial boundaries, the colonies federated in 1901. The new Commonwealth government was given certain powers relating to issues of tariffs, customs, defence, immigration and other matters of national concern. The state governments retained their individual powers in areas such as law and order (police, courts, prisons), education and social welfare, and internal economic management.

There was now an Australian nation which could conduct itself as one in matters of foreign policy and defence. Yet even though the Commonwealth government gained new powers in a formal sense in these areas, its policy in both continued to mirror British policy at least until 1942. Thus Australia followed Britain into battle when international rivalry finally erupted into the massive destruction of the First World War. Although this war never came anywhere near Australian soil, the loss of life amongst the troops was substantial. It was not until the Second World War, when Britain was tied up in the European war, and it was the

USA that provided the major military force against Japan in the Pacific, that Australian dependence on Britain in defence and foreign policy matters was decisively reduced.

Australia After the Second World War

It was also the Second World War which saw a significant shift in the Australian economy away from dependence on imported manufactured goods to the emergence of a heavy industrial base within Australia itself. There had always been a little light manufacturing in the colonies, and from the 1870s manufacturing had grown, especially in Victoria, behind protective tariff barriers. Some of the earliest manufacturing industries were in textiles and clothing; large factories were set up, and generally employed women as the traditional and cheapest source of labour. It was during the First World War, when Australia was cut off from supplies from Britain, that heavy industry was established (BHP was set up in 1915), laying the basis for further development of manufacturing industry. After the war Australia continued its role as a supplier of primary products to Europe; but there was also a continued growth in manufacturing, behind a high tariff barrier. British, American and local capital was used to establish many new manufacturing plants and industries.

This expansion was temporarily halted during the Great Depression of the 1930s. With the dramatic fall in the prices gained for primary products on the world market, and burdened with huge public debts to overseas financiers, the Australian economy went into a severe decline. Unemployment reached unprecedented levels, around 29 per cent by 1932. In this situation many small businesses collapsed, and the larger ones were forced to restructure their operations to reduce labour costs and increase efficiency.

It took the Second World War to stimulate real industrial growth. Iron and steel production was greatly expanded to meet wartime needs for armaments and aeroplane manufacture. And this expansion occurred with a greater degree of government economic regulation than had been experienced since the early colonial days

Australia emerged from the Second World War in a greatly changed world situation — politically, financially and economically. The old colonial empires, including that of Britain, quite rapidly crumbled, and were replaced by a host of new politically independent nations. The postwar period saw the growing dominance of the USA and the USSR as leading economic, political and military world powers, operating in a situation where a great deal of the world was dependent economically and militarily on either one of them. The decline of colonialism in the formal sense did not mean the end of economic dependence, political interference, and worldwide spheres of influence.

For Australia, military dependence switched from Britain to the United States. Economically, the dual dependence on overseas capital and overseas sources of labour was intensified. Foreign investment and immigration had both fallen to an all-time low in the 1930s, owing to world economic stagnation. Both expanded dramatically after the war in the context of a worldwide economic boom. But the sources of both were changing. Whereas before the war a great deal of borrowing from overseas had been government borrowing from Britain, after the Second World War the pattern changed so that American and British-based companies invested in local private companies, often taking them over. And the source of labour was less British than before. Since the British economy was itself on the upswing, it was difficult to attract British immigrants in the numbers required. Therefore Southern Europe in particular became a significant source of immigration.

But although there was a great expansion of the economy, there were some deep-seated problems. One was the high tariff barrier, which meant that locally produced goods did not have to compete with those from overseas; as a result, many inefficiencies in local manufacturing developed. Australian manufacturing provided relatively few exports, which continued to be mainly raw materials such as wheat, wool, dairy products and minerals. Furthermore, the ready use of overseas capital to get many industries going in the 1950s and 1960s paved the way for many later problems, including the drain of profits from the country, and government helplessness in the face of decisions made in the boardrooms of New York and London.

Governing Australia

Australia now has a Federal system of government, with a Commonwealth and six state governments each with their own areas of jurisdiction. Each government is elected through the system known as parliamentary democracy, where all adults vote for the candidates of their choice; the party or grouping able to gain the allegiance of a majority of members in the parliament, or its Lower House, forms a government. This majority grouping elects a Prime Minister, and ministers to head each department within the bureaucracy (public service). These departments must carry out government policy. The framework for departmental activity is provided by the legislation passed by that government and previous governments. The details of its implementation are provided by the government of the day.

That's the theory. In practice, it's a good deal more complicated. Governments find that departments, especially departmental heads, have considerable power and can obstruct the implementation of government policy to a considerable degree. Moreover, governments find that while they have powers to regulate the economy these powers are limited by the Constitution and also by the immense economic power of the large companies and corporations, especially the transnationals with their headquarters outside Australia. And again, governments find that there are limits to which they can enforce compliance to their decisions. They have the police and the military at their disposal but generally they prefer not to use them. If they want to be re-elected they must rely on a fair degree of popular support, and so must seek that support for their decisions.

Government will generally seek to continue the basic economic structure of capitalism, but will also seek to modify it in particular ways. Since governments must keep one eye on the centres of economic power (and on the military), and the other on the voters, they have a difficult course to steer. Their stability depends on the assent of both. If a government were elected which set out to damage the interests of the owners of capital, those owners, it knows, have enormous resources with which to resist. They can withdraw or relocate their enterprises, though of course they will probably not wish to do so. They can support the development of paramilitary organisations seeking to overthrow the government by force. They can rely on large sections of the mass media, owners of capital themselves, to wage an unrelenting campaign against the government. Only a government secure in the support of the military and of the bulk of the population could withstand these pressures. As yet, Australian voters have not elected such a government. Yet they know, through the experience of the mildly reformist Whitlam government, that such pressures exist. Furthermore, the political culture in Australia is such that voters do not elect such revolutionary governments. The option of radically transforming or ending the basic economic structure of capitalism does not appear to the voters to exist, or to be desirable.

The options appear to voters to be far more narrow. This can be seen from examining the views of the major political parties. The difference between the parties is not always easy to define, and each has been beset by internal differences, splits and crises. But in general it would be fair to say that the Labor Party has traditionally had a strong working-class appeal, links with the trade union movement, and a greater interest in government enterprises and government regulation of the economy. In contrast the Liberal Party has had a strong middle and upper-class appeal, links with business, and a greater emphasis on the need for government to support, and only where necessary regulate, private enterprise. The Country Party (now the National Party) has appealed to farmers both large and small, and has in most matters supported the Liberal Party, a key source of conflict being on matters of economic policy such as tariffs where the interests of manufacturers and farmers differ.

The group to which either the Liberal Party or the Labor Party might appeal is the professionally trained middle class. Its rapid growth in the 1850s and 1860s, and its frequent support for government as against private economic activity and regulation, laid a basis for growing support of the Labor Party. Yet in many ways its sympathies could easily be alienated from Labor. The changing allegiances of this class were important for the Whitlam election victories in 1972 and 1974, the Fraser victories in 1975, 1977 and 1980, and the Hawke victories in 1983 and 1984.

In practice, while each party has a clear basis of support, each claims to represent the interests of the entire population. The Liberal Party aims to attract working-class voters on the grounds of superior economic management, the Labor Party aims to attract middle and even upper-class voters on much the same basis. It has often been observed that the differences between the parties are more apparent than real. The constraints on any government come into play when a party achieves office: Liberal-National Party governments become involved in social welfare, Labor governments act to defend the interests of private capital. The foreign policy differences between the major parties have not been great, though Labor governments have leant, ever so slightly, more to the model of an independent foreign policy than have the Liberal/National Party ones.

The Australian Nation: Immigration and Ethnic Diversity

There are certain issues that are divisive and important, yet the divisions have not been very strongly along party lines. Two such issues are those surrounding the family/women's role/sexual morality, and those to do with immigration policy/ethnicity/nationalism. In both cases we see 'liberals' and 'conservatives' in each of the major political parties.

The first set of issues, those to do with sex and gender, were always troublesome in colonial Australia. Until 1850 the family-household system was not fully entrenched. Given the greater numbers of men than women, especially in rural areas, many European men remained unmarried. Sexual contact for these men was either absent, or with Aboriginal women, or to an unknown extent, with each other. Among the working class, both convict and free, sexual relations and cohabitation of men and women were often not marked by legal marriage, a situation that mirrored that of the British working class. Rates of desertion by men of their wives or de facto wives and their children appear to have been high.

By the mid-nineteenth century, however, households based on a married couple and their children had become more common. The middle and upper classes married, as before, and the working class increasingly followed suit. Colonial families were marked by their very large size, with nine or more children per married couple being common. Both squatters and selectors in rural areas had large families. Various pressures combined to lower this average family size by the end of the century. The compulsory education acts made children a liability for a longer period of time; the 1890s Depression reduced the levels of marriage and childbearing. Although average family size rose again early in the century, the birthrate declined drastically during the 1930s Depression. During and especially after the Second World War, the rate of marriage increased and the birthrate picked up, but the larger families of the pre-1890s Depression era were never re-established.

Underlying the post-war change has been a long-term process: continued industrialisation. This has meant that it becomes more sensible to earn wages in the marketplace to *buy* goods and services than to try and produce those things at home. Housewives who once combined childcaring, cooking and cleaning with domestic production — food growing and processing, making clothes, and so on — now found it economically unwise to do so. As women's wages rose, and as many of the things people now wanted were not able to be produced in the home, women were pulled into the labour market and out of the increasingly unproductive household.

This process is reflected in the rapid rise in women's workforce participation since the Second World War. Most of this rise is in the number of part-time workers, but it nevertheless represents a real change in women's ability to manage childcare and income-earning. As workforce participation has gone up, so average family size has gone down. Along with both changes has come an active feminist movement, questioning dominant notions about women's domestic destiny and role. This movement has sought to construct a role for women as a distinct force in politics, and to combat those sexual ideologies that articulate a notion that male dominance in both public and private life is 'natural'. It has been critical of the traditional nuclear family as being based on women's economic dependence, and therefore their unfreedom.

And yet, of course, both women and men as categories of people are internally divided in a multitude of ways — by class, ethnicity, age and political allegiance. Feminism itself has developed its radical, socialist, liberal and conservative wings, while its opponents can be found in all political corners, including those occupied by the major political parties. Feminists have, however, gained a little more from Labor than from Liberal governments, for an example on issues of equal employment opportunity.

Nor have the major parties differed significantly on immigration issues. This is not because these are matters for consensus — on the contrary they are quite diverse — but because the divisions that have emerged have not been along traditional party lines. Migration is a basic feature of world capitalism; in Australia we need to understand both its general, and its specifically Australian, characteristics.

We need first to distinguish between temporary and permanent migration, although a great deal of what turns out to be permanent migration often starts out as temporary. Temporary migrations are common in world history, as workers seek better opportunities elsewhere, in order to return home with cash in their pockets to enable them to rise in the social structure they know. Many of Australia's early officials were in fact temporary migrants, doing a job for a specified period before returning home or to another colony. Many middle and upper-class migrants were also temporary, seeking to improve their fortunes before returning home. But because of the great distance between Australia and her sources of immigration (mainly Europe, especially Britain), Australian immigration has taken on a distinctive pattern, somewhat similar to that in other ex-British colonies such as the USA. Most immigrants came as, or at least became, permanent immigrants. Some, as we all know, were forced to come against their will. Few working-class immigrants, whether convicts or assisted free immigrants, could ever afford to return, and many did not have a great incentive to return. The policy implications of this situation were clear. If immigrants came to stay, then they had to become part of the new society.

The basic perspective on migration from the early nineteenth century has been that migrants should assimilate in the dominant Australian society. The position was consistently that only people able to assimilate ought to be allowed to come. Assimilation meant that if you were not British, then you must as soon as possible become British: in language, political beliefs and practices, and cultural habits such as family patterns, religion, dress and so on. As a result, immigration policy was directed at seeking out those who, it was thought, could become assimilated and at excluding those who could not. This became a matter of cross-class and cross-party consensus from 1900 to the 1960s.

The post-war immigration schemes were inaugurated by the Labor Government in 1947–48 and then continued by the Liberal/Country Party coalition governments for one main reason: the shortage of labour after the war. There had been exceptionally low birth rates during the 1930s Depression, and economically there existed the conditions for great economic expansion if only sufficient labour were available. The Labor Government set out to attract immigrants. British immigrants were preferred, but were simply not available on the scale required. Australia would have to look elsewhere. And so a once highly British-exclusivist and selective country began searching desperately for non-British immigrants. This policy was sold to a rather suspicious Australian working class on the basis that these immigrants were necessary to build the new post-war economy, and also to build Australia's population so that she could better defend herself in future wars. The government at first tried to allay fears by promising that for every non-British immigrant there would be ten from the United Kingdom, but by 1948 it was clear this promise could not be sustained.

The government turned first to the Europeans displaced by war and living in refugee camps in Europe — 170 000 of them within four years. During the 1950s agreements were signed and less formal arrangements were made with various European governments. The intake each year fluctuated wildly with economic conditions, between 50 000 and 150 000 per year. As a result the composition of the population underwent a marked change — from over 97 per cent Australian or British born in 1947 to just over 88 per cent in 1976.

During all this change, where fewer than half the immigrants were from the United Kingdom, the policy of assimilation remained. Various government authorities put a great deal of effort into trying to convince the British and Australian-born that non-British migrants could and should be easily assimilated. There was much self-congratulation at the government level that such large numbers of non-British people had been absorbed and assimilated with little difficulty. This complacency was beginning to crack in the mid-1960s and was brought under question most forcefully by James Jupp in a book *Arrivals and Departures* in 1966. Jupp pointed out that non-English-speaking migrants in general were largely outside decision-making processes, and that far from a record of smooth assimilation, were suffering a great deal of distress unnoticed and largely unknown to the Australian-born and the government. He drew attention to the departure rate of about 16 per cent, which indicated clearly that all was not rosy. By the late sixties schools, hospitals and welfare services were increasingly forced to recognise that non-

English speakers required greater and more specific help than they were getting. Henderson's 1966 Poverty Inquiry, published in 1969, was important in changing public perceptions of non-English-speaking migrants from examples of success in Australia to victims of economic exploitation and of official and community neglect.

So the overall perception at an official and public level moved from 'successful assimilation' to 'failure of assimilation'. Migrants began to be seen as a 'problem' group in society. The Immigration Department began to extend its concerns beyond recruitment to assisting assimilation in a more positive way. In particular, the problems of educating migrant children began to be taken more seriously. There was a proliferation, especially after 1972, of conferences and committees of inquiry related to migrant and ethnic issues.

During the 1970s more diverse conceptions arose of what migrants should do in Australian society. The ideals of assimilation, and the recognition that non-English-speaking migrants might face special problems, continued. But to these ideals were added cultural pluralism, or what is now called multiculturalism. An early statement of this ideal was given by Jerzy Zubrzycki to the Australian Citizenship Convention in 1968. He still looked forward to the incorporation of migrants into the mainstream institutions and decision-making processes in society. But, he said, alongside this structural assimilation there was room for cultural diversity, especially in the maintenance of immigrant languages and the general study of European and not simply British culture. This was also the view expressed by the Immigration Department in 1975: that one could have ethnic (cultural) diversity and still maintain national (political) unity. As Jean Martin points out, this ideal meant that diversity would be welcomed and encouraged only in areas of life that could be seen as non-political.

But for some, multiculturalism had to move into the political arena. Ethnic organisations, which had been formed in the 1950s, began to make political demands. In the middle 1970s Ethnic Communities Councils were formed in most states to represent common ethnic interests in political debates.

Some people, such as Al Grassby, have attempted to argue that given our history, Australian identity is necessarily multicultural. This view gained popularity through the 1970s, but has not been entirely successful. Many Australians of British descent resent the apparent deposing of their Britishness as a core aspect of Australian national identity. They argue that the very great differences in the numbers and length of residence of those of British descent, as compared with other immigrant groups, need to be recognised; that Australian institutions and cultural practices are in fact British-derived. The multicultural position has served to convert the self-perception of many Australians of British descent from unselfconsciously 'Australian' to aggressively 'Anglo-Australian', as members of a distinct ethnic majority. It is on this basis, in part, that there has been criticism of the reduced immigration intake from Britain.

Yet the question of Australian identity can not be an easy one. On the one hand, there is the continuing tension between Aborigines and other Australians. When an upper-class speaker on an Australia Day radio program in 1984 opposed multiculturalism on the basis of the comparative longevity — almost 200 years — of British cultural and political institutions in Australia, she was answered by an Aboriginal speaker who referred to Aborigines' 40 000 years of greater claim. On the other hand, there is the continuing question of how immigration will affect ethnic composition and national identity. If we consider the magnitude of the change wrought during the last 200 years, there is no reason to assume that there may not be changes equally momentous in the next 200. It is this question of who shall constitute the human population, and what shall be the political and cultural features of Australian society, that gives immigration debates and indeed Land Rights debates so much of their tension and edge. It is this precariousness, too, that underlies the conflicting, almost Freudian, attitudes to both Britain and the United States as powerful father figures. If nationalism invokes 'imagined communities', then for Australians the issue of what to imagine is a complex and troubling one.

Further reading

Braverman, Harry *Labor and Monopoly Capital* Monthly Review Press 1974
Brenner, Johanna and Maria Ramas 'Rethinking Women's Oppression' *New Left Review* No 144 March/April 1984 pp 33–71
Broome, Richard *The Aboriginal Australians* Allen & Unwin 1982
Burns, Ailsa and Grieve, Norma eds *Australian Womens New Feminist Perspectives* OUP 1986
Connell, R W and Irving, T H *Class Structure in Australian History* Longman 1980
Curthoys, Ann, Martin, Allan and Rowe, Tim eds *Australians Since 1939* (in the series *Australians an Historical Library*) Fairfax and Syme 1988
Dahrendorf, Ralf *Class and Class Conflict in Industrial Society* Stanford UP 1959
Himmelweit, Sue 'Production Rules OK? Waged Work and the Family' in Lynne Segal ed *What is to be Done About the Family?* Penguin 1983
Humphries, Jane 'The working class family, women's liberation and class

Humphries, Jane 'The working class family, women's liberation and class struggle: the case of nineteenth century British history' *Review of Radical Political Economics* Vol 9 No 3 Autumn 1977 pp 25–41

Jupp, James *Arrivals and Departures* Cheshire Lansdowne 1966

Martin, Jean *The Migrant Presence* George Allen and Unwin 1978

Marx, Karl *The Eighteenth Brumaire of Napoleon Bonaparte* 1851

Marx, Karl and Frederick Engels *The Manifesto of the Communist Party* 1848

Reynolds, Henry *The Other Side of the Frontier* Penguin 1982

Sydney Labour History Group *What Rough Beast? The State and Social Order in Australian History* George Allen and Unwin 1982

Wallerstein, Immanuel *Historical Capitalism* Verso 1983

Weber, Max *The Theory of Social and Economic Organisation* Talcott Parsons *ed* Free Press of Glencoe 1964

Wood, Stephen *ed The Degradation of Work* Hutchinson 1983

Wright, Erik Olin *Classes* Verso 1985

CHAPTER THREE

Communication as an Industry

by
Helen Wilson

The slogan that 'we live in a communication and information age' is repeated so frequently that we may no longer be sensitive to its full implication: that is, that Australian society now is fundamentally different from Australian society even of thirty years ago. The process of industrialisation, desribed in Chapter Two, has wrought a transformation; in particular, the economy has been fundamentally affected by the emergence into prominence of new industrial giants, the media organisations. They are producers of the mighty new commodities: communication and information. Sharemarket booms can now be driven by communication industries as much as by minerals, or by banking. In Helen Wilson's words: 'what has been and is happening under capitalism is the industrialisation of culture'.

That commodification of communication and the industrialisation of culture have far-reaching effects on our perception and reception of messages and meanings. These are the commodities that play a major part in shaping our understanding of the world, and that in turn lead us to take or condone social and individual actions. If we wish to be critical readers of the media, if we wish to look beyond what seems obvious and commonsense, then at the very least we need to be aware of the industrial processes involved in mass communication, and their effects. The basic facets of these processes include questions of ownership, of production, of the technologies involved, of forms and structures of distribution with the related consideration of access, and the structures and processes of consumption. All these form an interrelated, closely meshed set of relations that are, finally, affected in specific ways by the role the state takes, intervening to a greater or lesser degree.

While the preceding chapter has provided an account of the history behind the present social, political and economic structure of Australia, and has provided terms in which to think about social and political structures, in this chapter we focus on a specific sector of that society, its economy, and its culture. What emerges is that questions of communication are always political questions, questions about social power, the power to introduce certain meanings, the power to gain access to meanings, the power to introduce new technologies to change the whole network of access to and of relations of meaning. Above all, this chapter insists that it is impossible to understand mass communication unless one is aware it is in every sense an industry, and com-

munication is a commodity — whether in the form of Crocodile Dundee *or in the form of information for the forex market. And as a commodity, it is exchanged in a market that is highly structured, skewed by differences of access due to differences of power. A naive approach to these commodities is possible; that is what the communication industries urge. It is entirely and detrimentally misleading.*

The Industrialisation of Culture: Communication as a Commodity

What are communication industries? The term 'communication' is so broad as to be useless in many contexts, but it can usefully group a number of industries (partially different ones at different times) which are related because they create commodities with meaning. This is an oversimplified definition, which applies more clearly in some cases than others, as the commodity exchange relationship varies considerably. It may involve the marketing of cultural products like books or records, or more complex transactions between industries such as advertising and television, or now, the computerised information industry and international banking. The commodity exchanged becomes more and more difficult to locate.

What is an industry? It is organised production for a market. That is, it always involves owners of the means of production (newspaper owners in the case of the press) and a workforce — journalists, editors, and (until recently) printers. Contrast this organisation with that of, say, a peace group putting out a newsletter when it can. Industries produce for a market, and this normally means for profit, to keep the business going at least, if not to expand it. Thus large-scale production is usually involved, with implications for the kinds of work done and how it is organised. The industrial production of clothing, for example, is organised differently from the craft production of artefacts, which may be sold but are not normally controllable by market criteria. Food is an even better example. It is easy to name dozens of food industrialists and to contrast this with domestic production of food and craft production in certain kinds of restaurants. It is also easy to think of borderline cases, like craft shops in a tourist resort, which point to the changing industrial status of many activities.

Many of the communication industries developed out of craft production — activities such as writing, making music, drawing, photography, acting and so on. Aspects of this origin often affect particularly the production of 'high culture' artefacts. For example, many people assume that classical music or literary publishing ought to be supported by organisations whose very reason for existence has become to produce for a market, when such activities are not viable in market terms. Some aspects of the culture industries are still craft based, for example the Australian film industry does not have the industrial base provided by major Hollywood studios (E. Jacka and S. Dermody, *The Screening of Aus-*

tralia). Very few Australian films make money and most have been subsidised by the state in one form or another.

What has been and is happening under capitalism is the industrialisation of culture, and this does not necessarily mean its degradation. What used to be the privilege of the ruling class in the eighteenth century, the music of Mozart for example, is much more accessible now, though hardly part of popular culture until the film *Amadeus*. Out of the earlier craft writing developed a very rigid fiction publishing industry in Britain in the nineteenth century, dictating the form and content of what could be written. Many cultural forms have developed out of leisure pursuits, such as music or writing, but now many kinds of leisure activities have themselves been industrialised, such as tourism. It is still possible to travel for education or leisure, but travel packages, including many services, can now be purchased before leaving home. It is a dynamic aspect of capitalism that as new human activities develop, new areas can be colonised. Kerry Packer, for example, industrialised the old English ruling-class sport of cricket (Bill Bonney, 'Packer and Televised Cricket'). In doing so he created a new form of this sport, one-day cricket, especially designed for television.

The communication industries may be classified roughly according to how their markets, or audiences, are constructed. The culture industries in a straightforward sense are the publishing, record and film industries, where commodities are bought and paid for in the marketplace. Film is different from the other two because a material commodity is not exchanged, and more people can view a film without it costing the industry more, to some extent. There are obvious economies of scale involved in book and record publishing, so that a certain number of copies produced covers the costs of production and thenceforth the item makes a profit. The small-scale independent record, film and publishing operations are not fully industrialised, but operate at least partly on volunteer labour and do not have the capacity to reach a large audience.

There are also, of course, the more traditional cultural forms involving live performance. Many of these are 'high culture', like theatre and opera; rather than being organised on an industrial basis they largely depend on state support, though this is clearly inequitable when many taxpayers are supporting activities they will never see the benefit of. In the case of popular music, it is closely tied to the record industry and to airplay on commercial radio, so that most performers rely on record distribution and airplay in order to get audiences for their live performances. Few Australian performers can ever command international audiences or have international distribution of records from an Australian base. Those who make it in this sense tend to operate from a base outside the country.

The commercial media of the press, television and radio are the best recognised category of the communication industries, and are distinguished by their dependence, partial or complete, on advertising revenue. Their output is mediated through the needs of advertisers. These media, historically related to other forms of popular culture, have traditionally had large audiences, for their products are free or next to free to audiences because the advertising revenue contributes such a lot to the costs. But advertisers are interested in consumers rather than in mass audiences, so they do not support organs that have a large audience if that audience is too poor to be able to buy advertised products. The demise of the *Daily Herald* in England in 1964 is often cited as an example of this phenomenon (James Curran, *Mass Communication and Society*).

Another important sector comprises the communication service industries of advertising, public relations and information. These do not aim their products directly at audiences, but have the primary function of providing a service to corporations in the same way as accounting, law or insurance do. Advertising is, of course, the dominant force in determining what kind of commercial media we have. Public relations has less obvious connections with the media or culture, but this appears to be an underestimation. It is clear that publicity, press releases and events staged specifically for the media are a very large part of what gets processed into news, and thus journalists' practice departs from the traditional values of investigation and truth seeking (Brian Dale, *Ascent to Power...*).

The information industry is the newest of the communication industries. It has developed because of the need for large corporations to control information. There is a drive to industrialise information, to control access to it through control of the means, increasingly computerised, by which it is stored and transmitted. Electronically delivered information has a very different status from a book, for it cannot easily be separated from the technology that contains and carries it. The large-scale development of the information industry has effects on more established communication industries such as publishers and news agencies, who see opportunities to expand into the selling or delivery of electronic information.

What is it to view something as an industry, in contrast to other approaches? It is of course possible to study the products, the output, texts, how they are constructed and how they construct meaning. This can be done in various ways depending on the object of study and one's objective in studying it. For example, English literature as traditionally taught chooses a narrow selection of written work, justifying this on the basis of notions of merit, morality or tradition. It pays little attention to publishing as an industry and thus cannot assess any contribution to the text other than that of the author. This promotes a romantic view of the artist, whose work often is refused by publishers or other entrepreneurs (because they are stupid or cowardly?). Nor does it explain why some works have achieved a lasting reputation while similar ones are forgotten.

There is a more recent tradition of thinking about texts which has no stake in preserving the distinction between high and low culture. Once high culture is looked at from an industrial point of view, it becomes very difficult to sustain the distinction, for it is clearly based on the creation of different kinds of products for different kinds of audiences, and not on a contrast between genuine art and mass industrialised culture. This approach, drawing on a variety of intellectual traditions, applies to an enormous range of texts and provides great insight into how they operate. It is still, however, a textual approach and needs to be balanced by adequate attention to the industrial aspects of culture and, more broadly, communication.

Considering the industrial aspects of communication involves looking at six aspects: ownership, production, technology, distribution, consumption, and the role of the state.

Ownership of the Communication Industries

Television is the most lucrative media industry, but this was not predictable when it began in Australia in 1956, when broadcasting was mainly done live and so required considerable resources. The first television licensees were the newspaper owners, Fairfax, Packer, and the Herald and Weekly Times company. Murdoch started the Adelaide station NSW 9 in 1959, and the expansion of his television empire is one of the most flamboyant cases of media entrepreneurialism seen in Australia. Television had become a goldmine for owners by virtue of the popularity of cheap (to buy, though expensive to produce) American filmed series.

These were family companies where media empires (or at least their beginnings) were passed from one generation to their sons. They jointly acquired a kind of legendary status as owners of Australia's newspapers, magazines and radio and television stations. They also acquired interests in other industries and other countries. But their dominance of Australian media was to be severely shaken in 1987, when a combination of events resulted in these companies losing all their television interests. Television became much more lucrative as the possibility of operating national networks emerged, and the prices of strategic stations rose astronomically. They were bought by a different kind of corporation from the traditional media owners. Bond Media, Qintex and Westfield were new capitalist companies headed by speculative property tycoons without a background in media, without even having roots in the established ruling class.

What do these new owners tell us about how television has changed? The unit of ownership has become a network rather than one or two stations, so television is now more national in its orientation. It is also more centralised, with programs from Sydney dominating the schedules around the country. The network owners are thus very powerful indeed, and it was in recognition of this that the Broadcasting Tribunal in 1989 found that Alan Bond was not a 'fit and proper person' to hold broadcasting licences. The conflicts of interest for such diversified entrepreneurs concern many people, for their interests in property, minerals, brewing and shopping centres must at times interfere with their media interests. How independent then can the media be, when they are owned by organisations with vested interests in so many of the areas they report on?

Capitalist organisations are not secure though they may have periods of stability and dominance. The financial press constantly reports attempted or successful takeovers, often in terms of wars and conquests, and there may be speculation about companies' ability to survive high levels of debt. The major media companies were heavily in debt in the late 1980s, and this made their fate seem uncertain.

Following his company's acquisition of the Herald and Weekly Times in 1987, Murdoch emerged as owner of newspapers amounting to about 60 per cent of circulation. Because of various legal problems, he sold his Australian television stations, Channel 10 in Sydney and Melbourne. But Australia is only one of the three countries where News Corporation now has major interests in the press and broadcasting, for Murdoch's empire is firmly established in Britain and the United States. Packer still has magazines, including the *Womens Weekly*, and some newspapers. The Fairfax company was divided and disrupted by family disputes and debt, with a number of papers closed or sold. After 'the carve-up' ownership generally was more concentrated than ever before (Paul Chadwick, *Media Mates*).

The advertising industry in Australia is largely owned by American-based agencies, which set up branches in other countries in tandem with their clients' move offshore, mainly in the boom period of the 1950s and 1960s. Advertising has been quite independent of other industries in its ownership structure, despite its close dependence on its client companies. However, now it is becoming less independent as large organisations like J. Walter Thompson acquire interests in other industries such as public relations.

Owners of information companies come from various bases in the USA, such as traditional publishers like McGraw Hill, news agencies like Dow Jones, high technology corporations like Lockheed, financial services like Chase Manhattan, or credit reference organisations like Dun and Bradstreet. The Australian company most advanced as an information processor is Australian Associated Press (AAP), owned by the major media proprietors. It is called a news agency after its best known function, gathering Australian news for distribution regionally and overseas, and gathering overseas news. But AAP is moving into the information industry, so that as well as processing news it also performs various other services, mainly in the provision of financial information for subscribers. It must be said, however, that news sold to media clients has always only been part of the operation of so-called news agencies.

A striking feature of the ownership of many of the communication industries operating in Australia is that they are parts of international organisations whose headquarters are in the USA. This raises obvious but important questions about Australian sovereignty and about the congruence between political entities (nations) and the economic realities of international free trade. But there are still forces for a greater economic balance within political entities. Many Australians decry the idea of their country as primarily a supplier of raw materials for industries in other countries. Rather, it could have its own range of industries employing the available labour force, thus reducing the dependence on uncontrollable vicissitudes of the world economy. This can also be argued for the communication industries, which are in many respects dependent and derivative. When there is a local market for products and expertise in their production, it may be up to governments to try to foster national industries if it is politically advisable. Australian unions, notably Actors Equity, have played a dominant role in campaigning for protection of the industries in which their members work.

It is important to have an international perspective, to see the patterns of imperialism, of domination and resistance, in communication as well as in other spheres (Armand Mattelart, *International Image Markets*). There has been a controversy within UNESCO for some years over the 'free flow of information' between countries. In the past this has been about the operations of western news agencies in Third World countries, by means of which a western perspective is enforced on Third World views of international events. So, if a western leader is in a Third World country, it makes that country more newsworthy in general, and relations between Third World countries become mediated through relations with the First World. Overall, Third World countries are far more dependent than Australia is, if western communication industries operate there and there are no indigenous industries. The penetration of First World products and communication industries may have more drastic effects than American cultural imperialism has had in Australia. Coca Cola and Colgate are transnational products that have been sold to Australians by the advertising industry, but in Third World countries the promotion of such products may change people's values and lifestyles as well as their practices of consumption.

Production in the Communication Industries

Who are the producers? What is the labour process? How is it controlled? What are the barriers to entry, the career paths? What kinds of values and attitudes are held by various groups about their work? What kinds of labour or professional organisations are there and what roles do they play? These questions can be asked of any of the communication industries, for their production processes vary greatly. The production process in making a film or television program is much more complex and diffused than in writing a novel, though this has in the past obscured questions about the role of publishers. Some communication industries are relatively well studied in this regard (though not often systematically), while for others it is difficult to find information.

The production of a newspaper can be observed by a tour of its plant, but extensive observation and discussion is necessary to understand journalism more fully. For example, the fact that newspapers come out daily means that journalists are often organised in bureaucratic ways, covering 'rounds' like the courts, police, the union movement and parliament. This privileges those institutions as 'official sources' and makes news in many ways predictable, even though news is thought to be about unexpected events. In the case of a popular paper, there may be a contradiction between the anti-labour views of its owners and the need to sell to a mass audience. Thus journalists have to do work in, for example, the coverage of strikes — framing and interpreting such events to mobilise the consent of the audience. Truly investigative reports are the exception rather than the rule, and this may be because the owners have their own reasons for permitting or impeding such reporting.

There have been a number of production studies of particular television programs, and these point to the diffusion of control and authorship through the various specialist inputs made to the complex division of labour. Television news production also lends itself to observation and analysis (see *Hazell, the Making of a Television Series*). The context of media production varies from country to country, and the context of television production in Australia differs considerably from that in Britain, where most such sociological study of production has been done. The major television stations in Australia have organised themselves into networks for the purpose of program buying or making, but they have done little program production themselves. The networks tend to contract 'independent' producers, so that they carry little risk if the program does not succeed (Albert Moran, *Images and Industry*).

For many industries, especially those which are highly capitalised like the film industry, there are few production centres in the world. Hollywood is the production centre for the international (and not just the American) film industry. Because large corporations are transnational, they can move production capacity. For example, the major world record companies operating in Australia looked to their local branches for increased production following CBS's American sales of Men at Work's 'Down Under' record in 1983.

Technologies of Communication

Technology is a very important factor, closely connected with production and distribution. It is often assumed that technology is an autonomous force because new developments in themselves have great power to effect social change ('television changed the world'). But it must be remembered that technology is not only developed but also deployed through political choices, within the framework of existing organisations and power relations. There are reasons why resources are allocated to research of specific kinds, and it is illuminating to look at the origins of our well-known communication technology. Radio was developed to overcome some of the technical and distance problems of telegraph and telephone systems, and was only later used for broadcasting. Similarly with television, which saw major development for military and surveillance reasons during the Second World War. Communication satellites came out of the American space and defence program, but their communication uses were designed to overcome the control held over international cables by the European powers. Broadcasting has thus been a side benefit of these technological developments, which were adopted for its use because political forces determined to do so (Raymond Williams, *Towards 2000*).

In western capitalist societies technology is not developed in any planned, overall way, with priorities being centrally decided before research allocations are made. Rather it occurs largely under the aegis of large corporations and is impelled by competition and the drive to enter new markets. When new technology becomes available for general use, there is much potential for struggle over who has rights to use it, for what purpose, and over how it can be controlled or regulated. There is a danger in adopting a viewpoint of 'technological determinism', which attributes particular outcomes to the technology itself rather than to its owners or managers, for it promotes attitudes of powerlessness and a sense of inevitability about current directions.

New technology potentially means the restructuring of industries and upheaval to traditional working patterns. Hot metal printing, long established as a trade, is now practically obsolete with the introduction of computer technology to newspaper production. Journalists' work has changed a great deal in the process (including widespread susceptibility to the debilitating effects of Repetitive Strain Injury) though the papers look much as before. Satellite transmission means that papers like the *Financial Review* can now be made up in Sydney and printed in Adelaide or Perth for local distribution. The next phase in the marriage of computer technology and publishing has seen the establishment of databases, containing vast amounts of franchised publications for consumers who have the technological means for accessing it. This in turn drastically changes the notion of public access to information and raises the question of the future of the print media.

Telematics, the interface between computing and telecommunications in systems such as videotext, is a big growth area with important ramifications for traditional communication industries, as the computing industry has developed with different assumptions from telecommunications. For example, telecommunications systems generally maintain a distinction between control of the carrier infrastructure — the telephone lines, cables, bearers — and control of the content that passes through the system. Computer organisations do not respect this distinction and have moved to control both as a package in their telematics ventures, in competition with the established telecommunications systems. When IBM established Satellite Business Systems in 1977, using satellites to transmit business information internationally, this was a direct challenge to the American telecommunications giant, AT&T.

Technologies and Systems of Distribution

The distribution of information and culture is largely determined by technology, and many distribution technologies are now unaffected by distance or national boundaries. In the case of print, a large number of copies must be stocked in a large number of outlets. Electronic publishing potentially eliminates such a transport operation (and allows for an international circulation of suitable publications).

Satellite technology has made live broadcasting possible over large distances to many outlets. Though there are possibilities for radically new forms of communication with this technology, few of them are realised. In television, satellites are mainly used to broadcast international news and immediate events like sports matches. A close look at the use to which international satellites are put in Australian news programs shows that they are largely delivering American-produced items, often without any kind of local processing or interpretation. So satellites come to be another channel for distributing American views of the world.

The traditional distribution of films through cinemas has broken down considerably, for cinemas now attract mainly a youth audience. However, there are other outlets for films — on television, in the video industry, and in some countries on cable television networks financed by subscribers. Control of film distribution in Australia by Hollywood interests has long been a stumbling block for Australian film-makers. It is an international case of a general phenomenon, namely that big producers also tend to be able to control distribution. It is difficult, therefore, for small or independent producers of films, books or records to distribute their products widely. They therefore cannot gain a mass market, though they may have a loyal or cult audience. In an industrial sense, they are marginal activities. In the case of records, the lack of distribution capacity means that records released by small local companies like Hot Records or Larrikin, in Australia, are very unlikely to be played on commercial radio, with the exponential increase in exposure and sales that that can promote.

The products of some of the communication industries are not distributed direct to the consumer, or to an outlet where a consumer can choose to see it. The output of the advertising and public relations industries pervades the established media, and it is to be expected that they will find ways of penetrating the newer outlets like video and videotext.

The Consumption of Media Products

Consumption is probably the least studied aspect of communication industries, at least by academic analysts. The industries do their own market research in order to find out how their products are being received. They often need to know the demographics of their audiences — age, sex, occupation, lifestyle — to know whether they can 'deliver' the right audience to advertisers. Some of this is instructive, and media people often have a shrewd understanding of who their audiences are, and of listening or viewing patterns throughout the day. In the case of publishing, companies need to know whether there is a demand for certain kinds of books, for instance in school or university curricula, and must keep a close watch on sales figures and make efforts to release books when the time is right, as for the Christmas market.

But market research cannot answer questions about what a particular program/film/book *means* to people, and why they consume it. While these questions are of marginal interest to market researchers, they certainly are of central interest to advertisers and PR people, who need to understand what makes some campaigns successful and not others. These are very important questions, for they point to what distinguishes the communication industries from other industries, namely that they produce meaning and shape consciousness. Since they do this on such a large scale, an understanding of how their products are consumed is central to any understanding of our culture.

What are the problems with studying consumption? It is very difficult to find reliable research methods where the responses people make are not somehow affected by the questions asked or by the power relations between the investigator and the subject. Any of the standard research methods used for quick quantified results have this problem. More satisfying and illuminating research would involve more time to establish a relationship of trust. It is therefore more likely to involve particular groups or subcultures, such as school children or a local community, with whom the researcher has contact over a period and for reasons other than merely the conduct of research programs.

Textual analysis may provide some valuable insights into cultural consumption. Identifying the structural elements and the codes by which they are linked gives clues as to what the texts mean to audiences. But texts can often be read in different ways and do not mean the same thing to all people at all times. The complex questions surrounding the role of texts is explored in detail in the next chapters, which deal with the structure of images, language, and texts of film and video. Here all that I wish to say is that in order to be comprehensive in studying the communication industries, it is necessary to develop sophisticated methods of empirical research on consumption as well as the methods put forward in the following chapters.

The concept of consumption may not always be applicable to communication industries, for it implies using something up, whereas much communication output is scanned, registered or looked at. Advertising, for example, is like this, and yet the need to satisfy advertisers can determine the consumption patterns of other media. The commercial breaks on television structure drama programs, and editorial policy in the press can become secondary to the demands for advertising revenue. The editorial material in the newspaper sections on food, travel, computers, or real estate does not contradict the content of the advertising around which such sections are designed.

This segmentation, or the creation of separate media outlets that target specific markets, also happens to some extent on television. In the late afternoon and early evening there is a dominance of advertising for sugar products, which angers many parents' groups. General food products and household items are advertised heavily in prime time. It is mainly women who buy these items and therefore they must be the target audience for the programs. Hence, perhaps, the replacement of crime drama by soap opera as the most dominant form of television drama. A professional male audience is assumed for the late night news programs, and, for instance, for the *Sunday* current affairs program on the Sydney television station Channel 9. These feature ads for computers, office furniture, business travel and the like. Though television is the major mass medium in terms of advertising expenditure and audience viewing time, it is in the interests of advertisers that the audience for any program be as homogeneous as possible. The high television viewing of groups such as the elderly or the unemployed does not mean that programs are devised specifically for them, for they are of little value to advertisers.

The State and the Communication Industries

The state has an important role in regulating communication industries, though many nation-states in the 1980s are weak in the face of pressure by organisations and interests stronger than themselves, even if they try to resist such pressure. Where there is a history of regulation, the state continues to play at least a co-ordinating role, but there is major dispute about how interventionist it can or should be between sections of the poulation with different interests in this.

There are various ways the state can intervene. It can protect national industries by establishing tariffs or quotas, or more indirectly, by financial assistance such as taxation concessions or grants. It is often noted in the case of the Australian film industry that, although production has at various times been assisted, distribution is not regulated, so that there is no guarantee that a taxpayer-funded Australian film will even be shown in Australian cinemas. Protection for the local industry has been a major part of television lobbying since it began, and there are quotas for prime time first release Australian drama programs on television and Australian music performances on commercial radio. The radio and tele-vision industries have consistently opposed these requirements, even when they have no difficulty fulfilling them, arguing that it hampers their freedom and forces them to broadcast inferior local material that does not rate as well as something already proven successful with over-seas audiences. This position is especially difficult for radio stations to sustain, for new records are generally supplied free to stations.

The press is comparatively unregulated in Australia, though owner-ship of radio, and particularly television, stations, has been closely con-trolled, allegedly to restrict concentration and monopoly power. However, the rules have manifestly failed to stop the development of organisations with formidable economic and political power. In Australia the state (specifically its statutory body, the Broadcasting Tribunal) licenses companies to run broadcasting stations for a limited period, after which it holds public hearings into the renewal of the licence. It is unheard of in Australia (unlike Britain, where the licensees do not own the broadcasting hardware as they do here) for a licence not to be renewed outright, but there are cases where conditions are put on it or where it is not renewed for the full term. It is debatable how much influ-ence members of the public can have on this process. Many groups have put considerable effort into making a case at these hearings about aspects of the station's performance. At the renewal of radio station 2GB's licence in 1982 the Sydney group Gay Solidarity made a case that the Festival of Light's Fred Nile had been offensive to homosexuals in his broadcasts, but the Tribunal eventually rejected this claim.

Because the stations always arm themselves with experienced and respected lawyers, and the Tribunal runs as a quasi-judicial body, the hearings can become inquisitorial. This may be discouraging for people without legal experience, especially when there is little ground on past evidence to expect that the Tribunal will take action on the basis of pub-lic submissions. The hearings do, however, have a valuable function in that they are in the public arena and provide an opportunity to observe industry executives defending their operations and policies. Some powers of the Tribunal were tested by court actions in 1985, and it could be expected that a Liberal government would try to curb its activities, since lengthy public hearings are seen as inefficient and wasteful.

The state also funds some broadcasting organisations and this practice has certain historical similarities with state support of high cultural institutions. The Australian Broadcasting Corporation (ABC) evolved on the model of the BBC as a vehicle for promoting high bourgeois culture, in contrast to the more popular commercial radio of the 1930s, though the ABC has always claimed to be about 'serving the public', 'providing a national service', and 'broadcasting for minorities' (Lesley Johnson, 'Sing 'em Muck, Clara'). State or public service broadcasters have thus been caught between the function of promoting high culture and that of being truly national, representing the diversity of the population. Conservative governments, especially since the economic recession of the 1970s, have been prone to reduce funding for such institutions and encourage them to seek commercial funding. The Hawke Labor government has not been very supportive of the organisation either, though it is hard to know whether the ABC has more enemies outside or within, for it seems to have a history of management difficulties, bad industrial relations and lack of direction.

There is in the 1980s a strong tendency, emanating from the USA, towards the deregulation of industry and the reduction of powers of government bodies. The large, diversified transnational corporations with interests in communications, like RCA, ITT, CBS, Westinghouse, Hughes, IBM, are so powerful that, even if a state is so inclined (as the Reagan government has not been), it is very difficult to regulate them. There are struggles in many countries over the privatisation of government instrumentalities whose efficiency as profit generators makes them attractive targets, but who are nevertheless portrayed as being less than efficiently run and capable of running at a profit for a corporation. Communications authorities are in the forefront of such struggles in various countries. The most celebrated is the Thatcher government's selling off of half of British Telecom to private investors, including its own employees, who then have a mistaken sense of participation in the control of the organisation. In other European countries the PTTs (after the French Postes, Télécommunications et Télédiffusion) are similarly under threat. It is not likely that a Labor government will privatise Telecom Australia, though before the 1983 election there were serious possibilities of it happening, with dire consequences for the quality of the national telephone service now run at a fair cost to all Australians. Under privatisation only the profitable sectors, such as long distance traffic for business would be developed. The remaining operations would then be unprofitable, especially since there might well be competition from satellite services. The issue, however, is on the political agenda of Labor.

Telematics has been developing mainly in the USA. There, computing has never been regulated, though telecommunications effectively has been by virtue of the arrangement in the 1930s under the New Deal whereby AT&T was allowed to run as a monopoly in exchange for providing an equitable universal service. The new hybrid industry has developed in a deregulatory context, and this raises questions about how telematics will function in countries, including Australia, whose PTT systems are still intact.

For Australia, mention must be made of the sectors which are marginal in terms of funds and audiences, but which are ideologically important sectors of state supported broadcasting: the Special Broadcasting Service (SBS) and public broadcasting. Both of these developments are unique to Australia, and both have enormous potential for democratising communication. The SBS broadcasts material from very different sources from other broadcasting organisations, though many complain that its television service does not pay enough attention to the many cultural groups in Australia. It is not well funded; nevertheless it has been expanding its television operations into other cities from its 1980 beginnings in Sydney and Melbourne, as well as running radio stations in those cities.

Public broadcasting was a daring innovation instigated by the Whitlam Labor government, and has been expanding rapidly in the number of licences issued under succeeding governments. One of its major achievements was to break the dominance of the airways by professional broadcasters with specially trained voices; its output has been a mixed bag, with some imitations of mainstream radio styles and some distinctive content and sounds developing, often in different languages. There are enormous problems in keeping such stations going when the state's support for them has been minimal, often just as grants for equipment and sometimes as indirect support through an educational institution. It is hardly an industrialised sector, and this is the source of both its strength and weaknesses. The lack of funding and the enormous dedication required to sustain voluntary work are difficult, and there is little unity in the public broadcasting movement, whose leaders have become preoccupied with the problem of finance and have embraced the idea of sponsorship as a solution.

AUSSAT: The Politics of Communication Technology

The introduction of Australia's 'domestic' satellite system, AUSSAT, has provided the most noteworthy recent issues affecting several communication industries, television being the most celebrated. The controversy over it has at many stages foregrounded the political processes involved in what many people would like to portray as a purely technical matter (Trevor Barr, *The Electronic Estate*).

The limitation on television station ownership and the fact that there is only one commercial station in country areas has long frustrated the major television owners, because this has limited the possible outlets for their programs. The networks would ideally like to expand to a national reach through affiliated stations, US style. This was behind the original interest shown by the Packer organisation, Consolidated Press, in the government establishing a national satellite system, an undertaking too expensive for one company.

The decision was made in 1979 on the rhetorical grounds that people in the outback could not receive television. Many groups, most notably the Australian Telecommunications Employees Association (ATEA), the union of Telecom technicians, argued that this was not the true objective, and, if it was, there were more economical terrestrial means of supplying television reception to so few scattered people. A more likely reason for the decision was provided by the fact that Consolidated Press found an ally in IBM, the parent company of Satellite Business Systems in the USA. IBM was the major partner of Consolidated Press in the similarly oriented group, Business Telecommunications Services, established in order to lobby for an unregulated satellite. This was a clear attack on Telecom's role in providing the infrastructure for live broadcasting hook-ups and business communication. It was an attempt to set up an alternative carrier that would allow the Packer group to network Channel 9, and IBM to transmit business information across the country and beyond.

The decision to buy a national satellite system never had a clearly stated rationale. It was always objected to by the Department of Finance because of its enormous cost, but this was overruled by technocrats. Despite its unclear purpose, decisions had to be made about its design. A 'flexible' system, having differently powered transponders for different purposes, was decided on, evidently on the assumption that the networks would lease the expensive high powered transponders, which have the capacity to switch from a national beam, covering the whole continent, to a 'spot' beam on one of the satellite's four 'footprints', requiring much less expensive receiving equipment on the ground. A great many decisions were made about the design of the satellite without consulting many potential users. The use the television networks could make of it was clear to many but never acknowledged publicly by the government. Telecom was strongly defended by the ATEA and its supporters (more than by Telecom's own management), so that the Liberal Fraser government never resolved the major uses of Aussat, nor its relationship with Telecom.

The Hawke Labor government inherited this very expensive undertaking, coming to be seen by many as a technological white elephant.

The ATEA again campaigned to scrap it (to which the government responded that it was too late) and then to have it owned and controlled by Telecom; however, Telecom was eventually granted only a 25 per cent share. It was by now clear that, having gone ahead with the project, the government had put the television networks into a powerful position, for it needed them as customers to get any substantial return.

The Broadcasting Tribunal was asked to report on the broadcasting aspects of the satellite in 1984. The Tribunal used this opportunity to investigate the structure of commercial television program supply. It identified a 'structural imbalance' in the system, with excessive power in the hands of the Sydney and Melbourne stations, who made all major decisions about which programs to produce, buy or axe. This finding was not in the networks' interests, and, by virtue of the cross ownership of television stations and newspapers, they managed to suppress information about the report, one of the most thorough and interventionist produced about Australian broadcasting. It made some radical proposals: that companies cannot both distribute programs and own two major stations, but must reduce their ownership to one station; that television owners outside Sydney and Melbourne ought to be encouraged to become new players in the game, so that network structure and satellite delivery would not remain in the control of stations in the two main cities; and that separate licences ought to be allocated for each of the footprint zones to broadcast a Remote Commerical Television Service (RCTS).

These recommendations did not suit the networks, not did the government embrace them, though it directed the Tribunal to allocate the four RCTS licences. While the networks were equivocal about using the satellite the government evidently had no inclination to displease them. It announced in 1985 that 'equalisation' of commercial television services had become its highest priority in broadcasting and undertook a review of the ownership and control rules, which looked at limits in terms of proportion of the population reached.

After much dispute, the government allowed companies to increase their ownership of television stations so that they reached a maximum of 60 per cent of the population. This implicit encouragement of national networking was quite opposed to the spirit of the Tribunal's Report. It sparked the upheavals in the media of 1987 as the 'new players' moved to take over stations in order to operate national networks using Aussat. Television ownership quickly became massively concentrated in the hands of companies new to the business. How successful these networks will be is yet to be seen. Questions remain as to their financial viability, their commitment to program development and production, and the future of any local input into their programming.

The satellite issue has posed questions about how television and radio could be distributed differently. For example, the Public Broadcasting Association of Australia (PBAA) discussed a proposal in 1985 for public broadcasting via satellite, which involved networking through the Southeast footprint. However, this proposal received criticism from some public broadcasters, who argued that networking and public broadcasting were contradictory, for this sector was intended to be local before anything else. It is possible to imagine a radical kind of networking in Australia, involving an alternative news service with 'uplinks' to the satellite all over the country, and therefore the capacity for live national coverage of events that are different from those the mainstream media cover. But the Aussat satellites are not designed with any such arrangement in mind. It will only be economic to uplink at the point from which the RCTS signal is transmitted, so there would be little advantage in the extra expense involved for public broadcasters, for there is already a national tape exchange.

The Aboriginal response to Aussat has been one of the most interesting. As the technology was announced as being primarily for the benefit of the outback, it was fitting for Aborigines to come forward to point out that they were a significant proportion of the outback population and ask how this expansion of white western culture was going to promote their interests. Aboriginal broadcasters are now active within the PBAA and have made many distinctive initiatives in broadcasting, including the gaining of specifically Aboriginal licences, 8 KIN and its associated translator stations over a wide area around Alice Springs. A subsidiary group of the Central Australian Aboriginal Media Association, Imparja, received the Central Zone RCTS licence.

So the introduction of Aussat has not gone entirely according to the original plans of the Packer group, and has proved to be a complex political exercise involving some unpredictable forces. It has proved to be an insoluble problem for the governments which have tried to deal with it, for it exposes their conflicting loyalties to the media barons who have displayed the power to seat and unseat governments, and to their own geographically scattered constituents.

Communication and Democracy

The communication industries are a recognisable sector of modern capitalism. Most have grown this century, though there were some important nineteenth century developments: books were made available to the reading public through libraries, and newspapers survived best if they had a cheap cover price and were funded by advertising. The expansion in markets for publishing and the press had democratic elements, as more people gained access to more products. But it also had anti-democratic elements. What was published became more and more determined by market forces, and the earlier diversity of the press was much diminished (James Curran, *Mass Communication and Society*).

Likewise, now there are democratic and anti-democratic elements in contemporary communications, though the picture is very different from that of last century. We hear a lot about the 'information society' and the 'information revolution' or the 'information age' that is upon us, all of which make this appear to be a democratic development. But writers like Herbert Schiller expose these phrases as rhetoric to help sell the concentration and privatisation of sources of information, in contrast to the public library model now being superseded. The new communications technology is very expensive, and though it can store and process far greater amounts far faster than the traditional technologies, so far it is much more restricted in access, and this is dangerous for any kind of democratic communication. Ways need to be found to open it up, maintaining and extending the 'common carrier' model of tele-communications.

The communication industries are a group because they are meaning-producing and this makes them important as objects of study. They are not a static group, but very much part of the dynamics of contemporary capitalism. The rise of the information industry means that the communication industries are increasingly linked to others, like banking, insurance and finance. It is almost certainly no accident, for example, that foreign banks are now operating in Australia, for the international information industry increases their ability to operate efficiently globally. This development complicates the picture, for it becomes difficult to distinguish a communication sector of the economy. Industries that were separate, like computing, are now connected with communication. The future of Telecom is now related to the television industry.

But equally, the forces of opposition are now uniting, and need to have a broader and more sophisticated understanding of the issues than such groups have had in the past. Unions representing interests as diverse as Telecom technicians or actors find themselves close allies with lobbyists for children's television in an organisation such as the Media and Communications Council, which therefore has impressive political and intellectual resources. Unions have been forced to analyse industries and to make thoroughgoing proposals for structural change or government intervention, which go far beyond the protection of members' jobs. In 1989 journalists from many countries organised a conference in Sydney called 'News Unlimited: Journalism and Global Ownership'.

The future of such a complex and changing industrial sector is difficult to predict. It is unclear how long the categories developed and the alliances described here will continue to be valid. Certainly, however, there will continue to be new forms of communication and, under advanced capitalism, this will give scope for further industrialisation.

Note
This chapter owes a great deal to the inspiration, questing and rigour of Bill Bonney, who died before it could be written. Greater detail on many of the industries mentioned here is provided in our co-authored book, *Australia's Commercial Media*, Macmillan, 1983. I am also grateful to Ian Reinecke for supplying much information and analysis, and for suggestions on an earlier draft.

Further Reading

Alvardo, Manuel and H Buscombe *ed Hazell, the Making of a Television Series* British Film Institute 1978

Australian Broadcasting Tribunal *Report on Satellite Program Services* AGPS 1984

Barr, Trevor *The Electronic Estate* Penguin 1985

Bonney, Bill 'Packer and Televised Cricket' *Media Paper No 2* NSWIT 1980

Chadwick, Paul *Media Mates* Macmillan 1989

Curran, James 'Capitalism and Control of the Press 1800–1975' in Curran J. *et al* eds *Mass Communication and Society* Edward Arnold 1977

Dale, Brian *Ascent to Power . . .* Allen and Unwin 1985

Jacka, Elizabeth and Dermody, Susan *The Screening of Australia* Currency 1986

Johnson, Lesley 'Sing 'em Muck, Clara' *Meanjin* 2 1982

Mattelart, Armand *International Image Markets* Comedia 1984

Moran, Albert *Images and Industry* Currency 1985

Munster, George *Rupert Murdoch, a Paper Prince* Viking 1985

O'Regan, Tom 'Towards a High Communciation Policy' *Continuum* 2:1 1988/9

O'Sullivan, Christine and Curry, Christine 'Teaching Television in Secondary Schools' *Media Paper No 6* NSWIT 1980

Reinecke, Ian 'Life without . . . we could have said no' *Media Information Australia* 38 November 1985

Schiller, Herbert *Information and the Crisis Economy* Ablex 1984

Williams, Raymond 'Culture and Technology' in *Towards 2000* Penguin 1983

CHAPTER FOUR

Language as Social Practice

by
Gunther Kress

The first three chapters have sketched aspects of the overall framework of communication. This chapter and the next two deal with the major media: language, visual images, and, in the case of film and video, a complex interweave of a large number of media.

Of these, language is the most common medium — all human societies have language, all human beings speak, barring some pathological condition. Perhaps it is because of that ubiquity that language is the most taken for granted, and perhaps the most overlooked. The commonsense assumption is that language enables us to express and share our ideas, that it is the vessel we fill with content of whatever kind. In that view language is a neutral medium, transparent and unproblematic, and ideas have some other existence before they are encoded in language. But those of us who know two or more languages also know the fundamental problems of translating from one language to another. It seems as though there is a very close fit of ideas and language; indeed, some ideas/forms of language seem to exist in one culture and not in another. Language and culture are very closely interwoven; social structures and linguistic form are intimately intermeshed. This is so across larger cultures, as much as it is the case in the social and cultural diversity within one society.

Every language reflects the values, meanings, practices and structures of the society of which it is an integral part. Language practices — speaking, writing, reading, listening/hearing — are social practices, often among the most potent social practices. Whether the pronouncement of a judge, or the promises of lovers, words once spoken powerfully shape future actions. The differences existing within one society, in the social groupings, gender differences, racial or ethnic variation, are reproduced in forms of language; and these forms of language are powerful forces in the constant reproduction of social difference. Differences of power among social groups and social actors within and across those groups are encoded in linguistic forms; they can be challenged, confirmed, reproduced, subverted, by the use of linguistic forms. Language is in fact very far from being a neutral carrier of meaning: it is language which constitutes meaning, and meaning is always and everywhere structured by differences of value-systems (ideologies) and by differences of power.

So this chapter is intended to show the forms and effects of language as a social practice. I will attempt to show how we come to be who (we think) we are through our experience of language, how we are positioned socially by language in the long or in the short term. I hope this chapter can give a first and useable insight into the structuring of communication in and by language.

1. Unsettling the Settled

The obvious has a way of being overlooked. And so it is that in many discussions about communication — whether in an informal chat or in a tertiary course — language gets no mention at all. Instead, there might be a lot of talk about strategies of interpersonal relations, about the effects of the mass media, about effective communication, or about communication behaviour in organisations, and so on; yet hardly anyone talks about the medium in which all this happens.

That seems strange. There are a number of explanations. Perhaps first and foremost, language — talking and listening at any rate — is entirely ordinary; everyone does it, barring some pathological condition, and indeed language does 'come naturally'. Reading and writing are exceptions to that, and many people even in literate societies never learn to read or write, or do so with great difficulty. As it is so completely a part of all our lives, we come to take language for granted and completely overlook its existence. Another reason is that being so natural, so available to all, language seems entirely transparent; we all know what it is and what it does: it is a medium for communication, after all. A fitting metaphor for that view would be that of a waterpipe carrying water, a conduit merely for the conveying or transfer of ideas from one individual to another.

So one thing I would like to do in this chapter is to unsettle some of these unspoken assumptions, to make that which seems natural seem strange, and to make that which seems obvious seem problematic. My reason is that as language is so fundamental to human culture and therefore to communication, it is worth understanding the role of that medium in our lives. Some of the notions I wish to challenge are part of common sense: that language is for communication, that language is transparent, that we all 'share' our language, that language is a neutral vehicle for the conveying of ideas. If these assumptions were correct, then the amount of time we should devote to the study of language ought to be very little indeed, about the same as the amount of time telegraph or radio operators devote to the study of morse code: not a lot. And yet language has been studied in all literate cultures for thousands of years, and it still remains a problematic field of study. There must be more to it than the commonsense view.

First then, what is it that we look at when we study language? Despite another popular view, namely that language is sounds and words or words and sentences, it is neither of these that we consider in a study of language from the viewpoint of communication. Human beings do not communicate in sounds or words or sentences. When we do communicate we think no more about words or sentences, let alone sounds, than we think about how far we should stand from our partner in conversation over a drink, or how or where we should sit at the meal table, or which eating implement to use, or what form of greeting to employ when we meet a workmate, or any one of countless social actions we perform at any one time in the course of the day. That is not to say that there are never occasions when we do not reflect on these matters. If we get invited to the boss' place for dinner we might become highly aware about where we should sit, at the table or anywhere; and in a job interview we might well become highly conscious about our vowel sounds, or the words we use. As soon as something significant is at stake those usually habitual social practices can become the focus for our own attention and monitoring.

Take, as an example, this admissions interview, conducted at a university in England, to determine whether to offer the applicant a place or not.

Dr Jones: The first thing I want to say, if you have any objection to this machine going on, if (inaudible) then kick it.

Brian Gentle: No, it won't put me off.

5   *Jones*: Good, fine, I'll try not to let it put *me* off. The things we go through for the sake of linguistics! Good. Let's sort you out, then. You are indeed Mr Brian Gentle, of (*candidate's address*). I thought I'd make quite certain (*laughter from Ie*) I've got the right person. (*Pause*) Er. yes. . . I don't know — School . . . and you're 18.8, which means you're really sort of the average age. (*Assenting*

10 *noises*) Good, fine . . . fine, then, have you been able to spend the whole day with us? Were you here for the Dean's talk?

Brian: Yes, I was. Yes, I was. And then I was sort of, er, had a look round, got here about half past eleven, er, then straight into the talk, and then sort of looked around the Library, and, er, the bookshops.

15 *Jones*: So, you've had the full treatment?

Brian: Yeah.

Jones: Lunch?

Brian: Er, yes, I had something to eat.

Jones: Which one? Down in the . . .

20 *Brian*: Er, yeah, down by the coffee bar.

Jones: Yeah, which one, the one at the end . . .

Brian: Yes.

Jones: . . . or fairly near the centre of the University?

Brian: Yes, the one sort of at the centre of the . . .

25 *Jones*: Ah, yes, a great place for chips and hot pies, isn't it?

Brian: Er, yes, that's right.

Jones: Good, then. Er . . . well, now that you've had, you've had a chance to read the Prospectus at some stage and then you've had the

Dean's talk, do you find the system, er, makes sense?

30   *Brian*: Yes, I think I'm, er, beginning to understand it better now,
and I must say, I'm quite sort of impressed . . . I quite like the idea
of, er, sort of flexibility, I think is the key word, isn't it?
. . . in the sort of Prospectus.

     Jones: So they tell us!

35   *Brian*: And yeah (*laughter*), and it seems to me as well, that the, er,
the exam system is, er, (*sounds of agreement from Ir*) a much better
idea, if you sort of, take it, the whole, the whole um, six terms,
and um, you know, work it out on assessment like that, rather than
sort of three hours, pass or fail, sort of.

40   *Jones*: How are you getting on with our *Don Juan?*

     Brian: Er, um, I quite like it really, it's er, part of it I find, er sort of er, a bit
contrived, but I suppose that's er, that's sort of Byron's
style, that er, um . . .

45   *Jones*: (*interrupting*) What is Byron's style?

     Brian: One, I think generally, he's er, it's um somewhat satirical
style in that . . .

     Jones: Uh huh (*general encouraging noises*).

50   *Brian*: . . . Uh, he's particularly in *Don Juan*, he's sort of bringing
out the, er, bitterness of his sort of family life I mean, his wife, er
left him on er . . .

(from *Language and Control*, pp 72-73)

Obviously a lot is at stake here for Brian Gentle (*not* the applicant's real
name) and he is therefore under very great pressure to choose his words
carefully. This is particularly so as his words, his use of language, are the
basis on which he will be mainly judged. That carefulness about choice
of language is shown by a number of things in this interview text: by the
great number of hesitations (much greater than those by Dr Jones); by
the great number of 'fillers' (the *ums, ers, you knows, sort ofs*); the uses
of *I think, I suppose, somewhat, quite 'quite sort of impressed'* (*line* 31);
and the tag-questions (*isn't it?*). Are these nothing more than signs of
inarticulateness? That certainly is one explanation often given when
people see transcriptions of speech 'written down'. But Brian Gentle is
one of the top 15 per cent or so of the population in Great Britain who
has made it to university entrance level; if we decide to label him as inarticulate what we will call the remaining 85 per cent of the population?
There is a much better explanation for his use of language here, and it
has to do with the structure of this social occasion and the way both Dr
Jones and Brian Gentle are placed in that structure. Dr Jones has the
power to make a most important decision about Brian Gentle's future, in
fact he has much greater power here than Brian Gentle. This power dif-

ference provides as plausible an account of Brian Gentle's use of language
as it does of Dr Jones's.

For instance, it is Brian Gentle who has to choose his words carefully;
consequently it is he who needs time to think, and so it is he who hesi-
tates much more than Dr Jones. Take for instance the passage from lines
15 to 26. It is a conventional and ritualised section ostensibly concerned
with 'putting the interviewee at ease' by showing an interest in his personal welfare. Brian Gentle seems to have great problems even with this
straightforward section: line 18 'Er, yes, I had something to eat' in
response to the simple question 'lunch?' and line 20 'Er, yeah, down by
the coffee bar' in response to 'which one? Down in the . . .'. However, if
we look at this exchange more closely we discover that Dr Jones is asking
questions to which Brian Gentle knows he cannot give honest answers;
if it is conventional to ask about a guest's well-being, it is equally conventional for the guest not to do other than assert his well-being; host and
guest are engaged in a mutually escalating game of demonstrating concern and asserting well-being. That explains Brain Gentle's 'Er, yes, I had
something to eat', (clearly he did not have lunch); and his agreement to
the two mutually exclusive descriptions of where he ate: '. . .the one at
the end . . .' (line 21) and '. . .or fairly near the centre . . .', (line 23), by
his carefully worded 'yes, the one sort of at the centre . . .' (line 24). Obviously he didn't have chips and a hot pie, but would not, in this situation,
feel able to say so. Here we have, then, an account that explains the hesitations, the *er*, and the *sort of*. Given his lesser power, the interviewee
must take his time over his answers, and when he can't contradict the
interviewer, he has to use the evasive tactic of the *sort of*. This explanation also accounts for the use of the *I think* and *I suppose*: they allow
Gentle to offer something as merely a thought, merely a supposition.
Both avoid the directness of an unqualified assertion: compare lines
31-34 'I quite like the idea of, er, sort of, er, sort of flexibility. I think is
the key word, isn't it? . . . in the sort of Prospectus' with 'I like the flexibility, which is the key word in the Prospectus'. The hypothetical speaker
of the latter might well appear as too direct, too assertive, not subtle and
not intellectually careful enough to the interviewer — and consequently
be failed by the interviewer on those grounds. What this means is that
Brian Gentle's language may be just right for this occasion: giving lots of
signs of deferring to the interviewer's greater power (and knowledge) and
yet demonstrating what the interviewer might judge as a careful and dis-
criminating mind.

Two important points emerge from my analysis. On the one hand,
language use is a very precise indicator of social structures and processes,

and on the other hand, language is always a social practice alongside other social practices. Here in this interview for instance, many other social practices are involved, from the complex structures and practices of the education system to the practices of the layout and furnishing of rooms (here an academic's office), to culturally specific conventions regulating social interactions (imagine Brian Gentle saying 'Actually, no, I haven't had lunch, I wouldn't mind a pie and some chips if you could get them').

Even at this relatively early stage in my discussion it begins to emerge that language is not a transparent medium. It takes a little analysis and reflection to discover what is happening in this interview; it is not immediately obvious either to us as readers of the transcript, and most probably it was not obvious to the two participants on the original occasion. That realisation also permits us to ask a question about language as a medium for communication. What actually *is* being communicated here? On the face of it the interview seems about personal details: lunch, the university's assessment practices and the interviewee's attitudes to them, and Byron's poem *Don Juan*. But I want to suggest that analysis reveals something else is at issue here: seen from Brian Gentle's viewpoint, Dr Jones' interest in the interview lies in establishing whether this applicant shows the right mixture of deference to authority, intellectual subtlety and academic discrimination. So Brian Gentle uses language accordingly to produce that effect. From Dr Jones' point of view the interview is likely to look a bit differently: he may be interested in discovering the candidate's 'intellectual qualities' and 'likely chances of success'. Above that he also needs to manage the interview; he has to make sure that Brian Gentle is in and out of his office in twenty minutes, that in that time all the conventions of the interview have been observed ('putting the interviewee at ease' etc.) and that he has achieved his goal of assessing the candidate.

Communication has become a more complex notion than mere 'transmission of information'. It includes aspects of control on the part of both: Brian Gentle attempts to control Dr Jones' reaction/assessment and Dr Jones attempts to control the interview for his purposes; and aspects of power — Dr Jones ostensibly holds greater power, but Brian Gentle is no mere victim either. Each attempts to position and reposition the other.

Language as Social Practice

What, then, is the object of study in 'Language and Communication'? Certainly it is more and other than words and sentences. It is an event, a part of a social event, and the outcome of that social event. One outcome of the social event is a text, the text of the interview. By that I don't mean the actual transcription of the taperecording, nor even the recording, for even if no recorder had been in the room at the time the text would still have been produced, though its continued material existence would not have been guaranteed. Nevertheless, that text would have been produced, and would have had its effect on both interviewer and interviewee. The interviewer would have written his (in this instance) report on the basis of that text — his recollection of the whole interview. The interviewee would have reported (on) this text — to his schoolmates, his parents (perhaps), his teachers. For both interviewer and interviewee this interview text would have left some effect, however slight, on their future language practices and other social practices.

The object of study is therefore two things: the linguistic processes, which are a part of the social occasion of the interview and seen as one kind of social process in the context of, and in combination with, other social processes in the interview, and the outcome, the resultant text, which is the concrete (whether materially recorded or not) effect of the social structures at work in the interview. The emphasis on both the processes and the product are quite essential. The former allows us to understand the possibilities of language in socially constructed interactions. It gives us an idea how people, as social actors, can use language, can interact, how they experience possibilities and constraints. Above all, the focus on processes allows us to understand the complexities of communication. The emphasis on the product is equally essential. Not only because it gives academics the chance to study communication, but particularly because the product, the text, is an instance of the system on which communication is founded, and it provides a record of what the state of that system is at a particular time and in particular social situations. The emphasis on the processes is an emphasis on the possibilities of communication by people in actual interactions in time and history; the emphasis on product is an emphasis on the constraints exercised by the systems of communication, language included.

The important point to emerge is that language always occurs as text, and not as isolated words and sentences. From the standpoint of the study of communication the text is the significant unit of language; it is the material form of language. As the interview text above showed, texts are constructed with specific purposes: in this case by two speakers, in other cases by more participants, or, at times, by single writers. The purposes of the participants find their expression in every aspect of the form of a text. Consequently, any serious attempt to understand communication has to pay regard to every aspect of a text.

With this in mind I will consider another text, the front page of a community newspaper (figure 4.1). It comes from the inner Sydney suburb of Newtown. This suburb has in the last three decades seen a change from a lower working-class population to a large-scale influx of mainly Southern European immigrants from the latter half of the fifties, a strong student population due to its low-cost housing, and, from the mid-seventies an increasing trend both towards gentrification with a significant inflow of professional middle-class residents, and a large second wave of this time South-East Asian immigrants.

What does this text tell us about the social occasion in which it arose? About its producers? About their perception of their audience? First I want to stress that although this front page has messages in different languages, which we may want to think of as distinct and different texts (and, on my earlier definition, can do so), the page as a whole — and indeed the paper as a whole — can be treated as one text, and that is what I intend to do first. A number of points emerge immediately. The text consists of sections written in three different languagues: Serbo-Croat, English and Greek. This points at once to the multi-ethnic constitution of the readership, of the community. The fact that these three languages are chosen and not others points, perhaps, to their predominance in this community. Further, 'community' is here clearly not defined by or identified with a homogeneous language-grouping, as it often is.

The paper is called the *Newtown Voice*, not the *Argus* or the *Chronicle* or the *Recorder* or the *Herald* or *Mercury* or the *Advertiser*. Even though the names of newspapers tend to be cliches, that is, words or phrases that are thought to carry no real significance, nevertheless when a name is chosen for a new publication the significance of the name enters into the calculations of its likely effect, impact and readership. So *Voice* connotes the immediacy of the direct, spoken, informal, neighbourly interaction, the domain of the homely and private rather than that of the official and public, something that *Chronicle* for instance would not. We all have a voice, and believe that we can and should make our voice heard. Not all of us are chroniclers or recorders. There is nevertheless a paradox in the use of the name. It asserts that this socially, culturally and ethnically diverse suburb has a single voice, or that a single voice can speak for it. Clearly this is an attempt to transcend such diversity and difference, and appeal to a greater unity, to redefine what it is that constitutes a sense of community. In this laudable attempt the very real differences and their differential effects on the people living in Newtown are quite covered over. The name clearly has an ideological function, in the sense that it is an attempt by one group to achieve a particular point of view, which is

NEWTOWN VOICE

free   community   newspaper. 4

Kućno smeće se može ponovno iskoristiti na više načina:

Jedan od ovih servisa je po-duzeće ENTERPRISES, koje sa-kuplja jednom u mesecu alum-inijaste konzerve, boce i tegle, u Newtownu i Marrick-villu. Ako očete saznati koji dan u mesecu sakuplj-aju možete ih nazvati na telefon 51-4149. Poduzeće SMORGANS u St.Peter's sku-plja kartone i novine i nji-hove tel. broj je 519-5113. Konačno stare štofove, krpe i ostali tekstil sakupljaju dobrotvorne organizacije, kao St.Vincent de Paul i Smith Family. Možete i pro-dati u trgovine koje se bave preprodajom. U Newtownu ima dosta staretinarnica. Isto tako stari nameštaj možete prodati ili pokloniti gornjim dobrotvornim organizacijama.

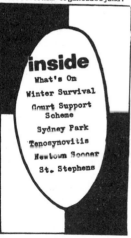

inside

What's On

Winter Survival

Court Support Scheme

Sydney Park

Tenosynovitis

Newtown Sooner

St. Stephens

WHAT A LOAD OF

Living in the inner city seems to go hand in hand with living next to waste and dirt. Much of what is thrown out can easily be re-used. Davies Enterprises, does a monthly collection of aluminium cans,glass bottles and jars in the Newtown/Marrickville area.For the exact date of collection in your street you can contact them on 514149. Smorgans at St. Peters, deals mainly with cardboard and newspapers. Enquiries can be directed to 5195113.Finally old cloth-es, rags and textiles can be taken to charitable organisations such as the Smith Family or St. Vincent de Paul, or perhaps sold to one of the many thriving second hand stores in Newtown. Furniture falls into the same category and places like S.V.D.P. run pick up services to collect what you give them.

RUBBISH !

ΠΩΣ ΝΑ ΑΞΙΟΠΟΙΗΤΕ Ο,ΤΙ ΑΥΡΗΣΤΟ ΕΧΕΤΕ

'Ολα τα άχρηστα αντικεί-μενα από το σπίτι σας μπορούν να ξαναχρησιμο-ποιηθούν με τον τρόπο της επαναγκυκλοφορίας των. 'Ένας τρόπος είναι μέσω της εταιρίας DA"I-EN που κάθε μήνα μαζεύ-ει αλουμινένια τενεκεδά-νια, μπουκάλια και κανά-τες στις περιοχές NEWTO-WN και MARRICKVILLE. Για να εξακριβώσετε πιά μέρα πεονούν από τη δι-εύθυνσή σας τηλεφωνήσα-τε στον αρι.θ. 514140.

Για περιπτώσεις χαρτο-κυβωτίων και εφημερίδων τηλεφωνήστε στον αρι.θ. 519 5113 στην εταιρία SMORGAN που είναι στο ST. PETERS.

Τέλος για φορέματα, ράκκοι, ή οτιδήποτε υφά σματα απωτανθήτε στα φι-λανθρωπικά ιδρύματα SMI-TH FAMILY ή ST. VINCENT DE PAUL ή μπορείτε να τα πουλήσετε σε ένα απ' τα SECOND HAND μαγαζιά γύρω στην περιοχή του NEWTOWN.

Front page of the Newtown Voice, *a community newspaper*

at odds with what can be seen to be the situation and with what may be in the better interests of the population of Newtown.

This contradiction between the assertion of unity and the reality of difference is illustrated by two other aspects of this text. The first is the fact that it is a free community newspaper — and hence available to all, irrespective of their ability to pay. The second is perhaps less obvious. Despite the assertion of 'unity in difference', the three languages are set in distinctly different type. English is the only one set in print; both Serbo-Croat and Greek are typed on a typewriter, with the Greek showing the poorest quality of reproduction. Thus in a quite trivial feature a very significant difference between the material resources available to the different groups is communicated. Again, as with the interview, that meaning is not intentionally signalled, but it is nonetheless a part of the meaning communicated by this text.

These contradictions are there in the language used in the brief texts, or at least in the English text, the only one I can read. To see this I need to engage again in some detailed and small-scale analysis of the actual language. This time I will look at aspects of grammar in order to make my point. Consider the first sentence: 'Living in the inner city seems to go hand in hand with living next to waste and dirt'. The main verb here is difficult to define; it is *seems* on first glance — 'something seems the case.' In terms of meaning the main verb is *go* — 'Living in the inner city goes hand in hand with . . .' I think the real action is not expressed by either, but by *living* (formally called a gerund or verbal noun). Living is what the action of this sentence is really about. Every verb needs a subject: *who* is doing it? Who is doing this *living*? The answer that the writers would give, and no doubt had in mind is 'all of us'. Consider, however, the second sentence: 'Much of what is thrown out can easily be re-used'. Here there are two verbs *thrown out* and *re-used*. Who are the subject/agents of these verbs? All of us? Probably not. Furthermore, are the subject/agents of *thrown out* the same as those of *re-used*? Again, probably not. Although I live in Newtown, and throw out what I consider rubbish, I do not re-use anyone else's thrown-outs. It may well be that the producers of this paper are quite like me in that respect; and they may be aware of that systematic distinction between those who throw out and those who re-use. To move a little further: the *you* of 'your street' and 'you can contact them . . .' is ambiguous. Does it include all of us, or is it only directed to the throwers-out? Similarly with the absent subject/agent in '. . .old clothes . . .can be taken . . .or perhaps sold. . .'.

In other words, at some level the reality of the social differences of Newtown reasserts itself, despite the writers' best efforts to elide them in

their text. More could be said about this front page and what it communicates, but I hope I have said enough to provide some answer to my
initial questions. What is the social occasion from which this text arose?
It is that of a socially and ethnically diverse community, living in one
geographically definable area, in which some members — definable in
terms of class and ethr city — come together in order to address problems that they perceive? Who are the producers? Well, as I have just said,
they are a socially and ethnically specifiable group who clearly understand the social and ethnic complexities of the suburb, who wish to
advance a particular view of community — one which transcends class
and ethnic difference — and who wish to do something for another
group, defined as different from themselves in terms of social class. This
also answers my last question, about their perception of their audience.

In my view, without the notion of text as the result of language processes in specific social contexts it would have been impossible for me to
ask these questions about the meaning of this text, and about its effect
in communication.

Speech and Writing: The Spheres of the Public and the Private

In my discussion of the *Newtown Voice* I pointed out the meanings that
attach to 'voice': meanings that cluster around spontaneity, informality,
authenticity, the neighbourly, and of the private rather than the public.
Some or all of these meanings adhere to speech, in the opposition of
speech and writing that is a feature of literate cultures. Of course, not all
cultures do have writing and not all languages have a writing system, and
therefore do not occur in the written mode. In English, writing and
speech are fundamentally related; both make use of the basic syntactic
unit of the clause. But writing and speech make significantly different
uses of this basic unit. Generalising somewhat here, in writing, clauses
are put together in often very complex ways to form sentences; in speaking clauses tend to be put together in equally complex but quite different
ways in what I shall call 'chains of clauses'. I'll illustrate this difference
with extracts from two texts about the same issue, namely the proposed
construction of a water storage dam on the upper Williams River,
northwest of Newcastle, NSW. The first, the spoken text, is from an
interview with a local resident; a woman in her early eighties who has
lived and worked for most of her life on a dairy farm in the area. The second, the written text, is from a letter written by the State Minister for
Natural Resources to a resident.

Spoken Text

1   ... and ah/... we're down like/further/... but they said at
the time/... it'd be seven acres/they thought that they'd
be taking of ours/down there like/you know/that was a good
while ago/... well/... whether whether they came here/oh/...
5   look/I forget/... and ah Perce went round with them/or
whether they came here/and ... judged for themselves/I
don't know/but they never looked in the house/... if/... if
they did come here/they didn't come to the/... come in
the house/or anything/......
10   ... and ah/...well/whether they will come/or whether they
won't come/or when they're ready to come/I don't know/...
'spose they'll notify us/but oh we've had/... oh/... had
letters from them/... but ohh gosh/eh/... they/... well
the letters they write are away over your head/... you
15   know/er/... about this/and about something else/... well
I said to Perce/well look let the/... let the tail go with
the hide/I said if they want the place/they'll take it/
and if they don't want it/well we'll still live here/
... we're not going to worry about it/
(The oblique strokes indicate the boundaries of 'sense-groups'; the dots indicate
relative length of pauses).

Written Text

1   Dear Ms Sylvia
I am writing to acknowledge your further letter in regard to the
proposed Tillegra Dam.
I share your concern for losses to the local dairy and beef
5   industries which will arise from future dam construction at Tillegra. You must
appreciate however that the Government is
obliged to take into account *all* the likely effects of each
alternate proposal when making any decision with such far
reaching consequences. Economic, social and environmental
10   impacts must be examined not only on a local base but regionally
and, if applicable, at a State wide level. Not the least of
these considerations is the need for an economical and reliable
source of water to the people and industry of the Lower Hunter.
The decision favouring Tillegra was based on the widest
15   considerations. The Government has accepted that Tillegra is the
right choice. You may of course be assured that every effort
will be made to minimise negative impacts of the scheme.
In comparing the Johnsons Creek/Karuah option with Tillegra, the
results of broad based consideration indicated that the overall
20   impact on the environment was similar if not somewhat greater for
the Johnsons Creek/Karuah case than for Tillegra. On a simple
economic comparison the result was quite clear, with costs

favouring Tillegra by 38% on a discounted cash flow basis and by
18% on the unit cost of production of water.
25   The alternative which you mention, construction of a large dam at
Chichester, has been examined in detail. The existence of an
ancient landslide area above the left abutment of the present dam
has posed serious doubts about the safety of any structure with a
significantly higher water level. Even if an engineering
30   solution could be found the costs involved would be prohibitive.
Part of the overall scheme for the Tillegra project does include
the priority enlargement of the existing Grahamstown Reservoir.
Raising the full supply level at Grahamstown by about 1.5 metres
will add some 36,000 megalitres or twice the capacity of
35   Chichester Dam. This additional water will be drawn from the
existing flow of the Williams River, which will later be
supplemented by water stored at Tillegra.

The difference is starkly apparent, though what that difference is about
may not be as obviously clear. I will give a brief characterisation of each
of the two textual extracts in order to establish what the meanings and
possibilities of speech and of writing are, and how they fit into a larger
cultural setting.

Speech typically occurs in the context of immediate interaction, in the
presence of the person or persons spoken to. This means that the audience of spoken language tends to be known to the speaker, and quite frequently both speaker and addressee are familiar with the context. Here
for instance, much of the speech makes direct though not very explicit
reference to aspects of the context: 'we're down like' (line 1) where the
addressee knows both who 'we' are (the woman and her husband) and
where 'down like' is (downstream from a particular point on the
Williams River); 'they said at the time' (lines 1-2) where the identity of
'they' is known (people from the Waterboard) and 'at the time' is a reference to a time known to speaker and addressee; 'they'd be taking of ours/
down there like' (line 3) — here 'ours' is 'our farming land' and 'down
there' is land close by the river. The point is that much knowledge is
shared by speaker and hearer and therefore does not have to be made
explicit but can be (indeed generally has to be) left implicit. That very
fact establishes a vast area of common ground for speaker and hearer, a
shared world.

The joint presence of speaker and hearer also accounts for a fundamental aspect of the structure of speech. I mentioned above that I had indicated 'sense-groups' in the transcribed speech. These are clearly
indicated in speech through the resources of the spoken language, in particular through the 'ups and downs' of the voice, the rises and falls in

pitch which are called intonation. Speakers mark off each sense-group by giving it a single intonation contour, including one highly pronounced pitchmovement. For instance 'we're *down* like' with a fall from high to low pitch on *down*; or 'it'd be seven *acres*' with a fall in pitchmovement on *acres*; and so on. These sense-groups and their pitchmovements give a highly articulated and finely pronounced guide to the listener about the meaning-structure of the spoken communication, in fact, telling the listener how to hear or understand the message.

In other words, the very structure of speech is oriented towards facilitating and guiding the hearer's understanding. That also explains the interspersed *wells*, *you knows*, *ohs* and *goshs*. They provide little clues about the speaker's attitude, now summing up and pointing forward (well), now calling on the listener to provide tacit agreement through an appeal to shared knowledge (you know), now signalling particular emphasis (oh) and astonishment (gosh). Superimposed on all this is a subtly constructed mesh of logical connections, say, from lines 1 to 10: *and* (co-ordinating link) . . . *but* (partially negating link) . . . *it'(woul)d* (hypothetical statement) . . . *they' (woul)d* (hypothetical statement) . . . *whether* (possibility of doubt) . . . *or whether* (alternative) . . . *and* (co-ordinating link) . . . *but* . . . *if/(then)* (hypothetical condition).

The argument develops through the successive linking of simple clauses, i.e. structures of subject noun, verb and complement. For instance 'we're down like', where *we* is the subject, *are* is the verb, and *down* is an associated circumstance, i.e., indicating the place where this *is*. Or, 'but they said at the time', where *but* is the link with the preceding speech, *they* is subject, *said* is the verb, and *at the time* indicates the time when this happened. Or 'I forget' with *I* as subject and *forget* as the verb. So in all this there is a most complex structure of successive clauses linked in a complex mesh of logical linkages tied together in a finely woven texture of intonational meaning-guide, and the interspersed pointers of the speaker's attitudinal position.

Despite this great complexity speech is and remains essentially spontaneous. Where spontaneity is not possible, then informal, casual speech also becomes impossible. Because casual speech is so spontaneous there is no or very little time for review, for deliberateness, for censorship. Consequently, where it becomes necessary to exercise care and to review what is being said, the forms of casual speech disappear. It is a particular skill to monitor one's own speech carefully and to remain articulate, a skill not everyone is trained to develop; so that in many situations where much is at issue many speakers, those who do not have that ability, have to remain silent.

Writing is the antithesis of spontaneity. Writing is deliberate in every way. It is the domain of review, editing, censorship, recasting. While speech is immediate in many ways, writing is distant in equally many ways. The writer tends to be distant from her or his addressee; and with the physical absence of the addressee tends to come a distance from the addressee in other ways. Writers, typically, know much less about their audience than speakers do. And so the writer's focus tends to move away from the addressee and turns instead to the subject matter. While the structure of speech is ultimately determined by the speaker's need to focus on the hearer, the structure of writing is ultimately determined by the writer's need to control the subject matter. And as the immediate context of writing becomes less important (for instance, does this text give you any clue as to whether it was written in the daytime or the night time, in my home or my office at work; does it tell you how far my office is from my home 'down there like, in Newtown'?), so there is an increasing distance also from the subject matter. Unlike the subject matter of the speech above, it is not connected to the immediately proximate environment.

What does all this mean in relation to the Minister's letter? The Minister, in writing this letter, is in very many ways at a great distance from the addressee of the letter. Indeed it is highly unlikely that the Minister wrote this letter at all, but rather had someone write the letter for her, or perhaps even more accurately, would not even have been aware of the fact that a letter was being written on her behalf. This is an apt metaphor for the distance between writer and reader. The Minister and the addressee cannot refer to a shared immediate context. Rather, that has to be explicitly established — 'the proposed Tillegra Dam', 'I share your concern', 'losses to the local dairy . . . industries', 'future dam construction', and so on. After the initial naming of the Minister of herself with the *I*, that index of personal involvement quickly disappears to be replaced first by the collective *the Government* (line 6), and then by the agentless passive forms of '. . . impacts must be examined' (line 10), '. . . was based' (line 14), ' will be made' (line 17), where in each case presumably it is the government or some instrumentality that is the subject/agent. My point here is not so much that the sources of action or responsibility become increasingly blurred or invisible, which is the case, but rather there is an increasing effacement by the writer from the text. The writer's own actions become blurred and invisible and blend in with the actions of abstract and collective institutions, whose agency is not acknowledged. For instance, in lines 14-15 'The decision favouring Tillegra was based on the widest considerations', we are left to puzzle about what was actually done by whom and on whose behalf. As the woman speaker says, 'but ohhh gosh eh . . . they . . . the letters they write are away over our head . . . you know er . . . about this and about something else'. If we attempt to unpick this sentence, what we will find is both considerable complexity and a remaining sense of bafflement. So for instance, it wasn't an individual, a group, or even a governmental department that favoured Tillegra, but a 'decision'. We know, as language users, that the noun *decision* is related to a clause such as *someone decided something*, but we certainly cannot recover who or what. Similarly with 'the widest considerations'; again we know that *consideration* is related to *someone considered something* (widely), though again we are left entirely baffled about who considered what, and about what 'widely' might mean here. Nor are we given any indication about who it was that based one decision on the other ('the decision . . . was based on . . . considerations').

Notice that this letter absolutely abounds with such constructions: 'future dam constructions', 'each alternate proposal', 'the likely effects', 'economic, social and environmental impacts', 'negative impacts of the scheme', etc. etc; or with even more highly complex subject nouns such as (line 26) 'The existence of an ancient landslide area above the left abutment of the present dam'. In the spoken text these are simply nonexistent. One difference therefore seems to be that writing favours forms in which actions — 'they never looked in the house', — (lines 7-8) become object-like, such as 'their looking into the house', or more likely 'their inspection'.

All of this is aided or even made possible by the sentence, that most characteristic feature of language in the written mode. For just as writing focuses the writer's attention on the subject matter, so the sentence focuses the writer's attention on the development, shaping and control of stages in an argument, on the coherent development of complex conceptual relations within one unit. So the ideas expressed in a number of clauses are put together and reordered into a construct that corresponds to the writer's perceived need in the development of a text. To take the sentence I considered just a moment ago. It contains at least the following clauses: *someone decided something*, and *that favoured Tillegra*, and *someone based that on something*, and that was that *someone considered something*, and *they considered it widely*. There are five clauses here, which have been compressed into one sentence, in an ordering that reflects the writer's view of the most appropriate arrangement of that material in the context of the wider argument. A translation into speech might be something like this: 'Yeah, and they . . . they decided to do it, and they favoured Tillegra, and they did that . . . er . . . because they said, er . . . that they had asked a lot of people, and they agreed with it'. So far my discussion of the written text may suggest that I consider the effects of writing as being entirely negative. That is not the case. For one thing, if you look over my text you will find very many of the forms I have just described. And while it is no doubt true that I am using many of them because I have been trained to write in that way, particularly as an academic, I also consider that in many ways there are considerable benefits in the conceptual technology of writing which I find essential and helpful, living in the kind of culture that I live in. Both the benefits and the drawbacks centre on that notion of 'distance' that I described earlier. Writing as a medium and writing as an activity both encourage and permit distancing — from the immediate context, from the audience, and from the subject matter. All of these permit a greater degree of reflectiveness and deliberateness; the writer is freed from the pressing contingent demands of all aspects of the immediate context. Perhaps the most important of these benefits, and one which meshes most closely with the demands of a scientifically and technologically oriented society, is the possibility of developing new conceptual tools — new labels and new configurations of ideas — which together give one kind of control and mastery of the environment. Labels such as I have described above — for instance 'the prior enlargement of the existing Grahamstown Reservoir', 'raising the full supply level at Grahamstown by about 1.5 metres,' 'the existing flow of the Williams River', — each label represents a complex of actions, judgments, effects condensed into a new conceptual unit which can then begin to function in its own way in new conceptual, political, ideological considerations or battles. In that way 'the prior enlargement of the existing Grahamstown Reservoir' can become a counter in this or another battle — for instance with farmers near that reservoir who may in their turn find that 'the existing flow of the Williams River' has to be accommodated by a compulsory purchase of a part of their land, etc.

The edifices of western science, technology and bureaucracy rest on the linguistic technology of writing. That is the gain. But that is not to say that science of a different kind, different technologies and different forms of bureaucracy could not exist without writing. The forms of speech imply their own science: they imply different forms of control and of interaction. The gain of distance is at the same time the loss sustained through writing. The benefits of the forms of speech are in its immediacy, spontaneity, fluidity, proximateness. While speech is closer to solidarity, writing is closer to power. Our culture has long oriented itself along the values of writing in its public situations and declarations, while at the same time maintaining romanticised images of the values of speech for the domains of the private. It is not the case, therefore, that our culture has ignored the forms of speech, but it is true that it has assigned them to the domain of the private, the domain of relative absence of power, the domain of the home, the domain of women, of children, of the lower classes, of pleasure and of the personal. There the forms of speech have been subject to romanticised fantasies of individualism, of 'real life' contrasted with the distortions and falsity of 'social life'. I need to say here what I should perhaps have said earlier: both categories, of private and public, are of course socially constructed. That is, I am not assuming that the private domain is somehow outside the social domain, beyond the socio-cultural. Rather, I regard the private as that domain which is socially constructed as an area that seems to be beyond the larger scale political and economic processes of a society, to appear as the domain of individuality, as that which is outside the social, the sphere of individual freedom beyond the contingencies of the social. The public is constructed as that sphere which is the domain of the action of social, political and economic forces, and of persons within that domain acting not as individuals but as social agents in social roles. Underlying this distinction is therefore an ideology which declares that the private is the domain beyond social theory and beyond ideology.

This leads to a quite common ideological twist whereby those whose lives are conducted largely in the domain of the private and who use the mode of language of that domain are at the same time deprived of power and told that theirs is the domain of real value. That neat trick has important ideological and political uses in confirming social persons in their powerless position. It is a device characteristically employed in certain of the mass media. The tabloid press, for instance, tends to represent events in such a way as to entrench that view. As an example, the Sydney paper *The Daily Telegraph* adopts a structure for its front page which, just about invariably, consists of two stories and two pictures, one for each story. So for instance, on 26 October 1985 the stories were: 'Di is No. 1 for Charles No. 2' and 'Baby dies in van blaze horror'. In the first story a public figure, Princess Di, is presented in terms of the private — a man from a working-class suburb of Melbourne kissed her hand; in the second story an event from the private domain — a young child involved in a fatal domestic accident — is presented as a matter of public interest.

So in the one instance the public is presented as essentially the (same as the) private, when Charles Opychral 'from the Melbourne suburb of Broadmeadows . . . planted a romantic kiss' on Princess Di's hand just moments after 'the royal bedroom, the RAAF 707 jet . . . landed'. Charles' girlfriend seems to have seen the event in private terms if the paper is to be believed; she is reported as not being too worried by Charles' encounter: 'I'm not jealous of him kissing her. I love it when men do it like that'. In the other instance the private is brought into the most public position in the newspaper, the front page, which is by definition the place where the most significant and most public events are presented. In an important sense that is what the paper is saying to its readers: 'Nothing is more important than the private, the world that is familiar to you; in effect there is nothing beyond that'.

The effect is to merge the two domains into one, so each seems to be like the other, and all events seem to belong to the same domain as that in which readers live perhaps the greater part of their lives. The political effect is to deny the existence of the public domain and prevent readers from developing accounts of social life, to urge them to accept that all of life is like their own private lives, where everything can be accounted for in terms of individual action.

Of course not all media organs act in this way; after all, different papers have different audiences. So-called 'quality papers' address a readership which sees itself very much in public terms, or at least makes a clear division between the two spheres. The *Sydney Morning Herald* for instance has a quite separate section to mark off the private from the public. So the former is given its own lift-out section, for instance, the 'Good Living' section on Tuesdays, the 'Guide' (a leisure section) on Mondays, or the 'Metro', an entertainment guide on Fridays.

To show how the two papers, the *Sydney Morning Herald* and the *Daily Telegraph* mediate the one event between the spheres of public and private, here are two reports (figures 4.2 and 4.3). They deal with the decision of the Arbitration Commission (a Federal industrial court) concerning the deregistration case brought against the Builders Labourers Federation (BLF) by the Victorian state government and Federal government.

The two reports concern what is ostensibly the same event, and indeed both may be rewritings of the same AAP report. Yet in one, the *Daily Telegraph*, the event is constructed in terms of the private domain, whereas in the other, the *Sydney Morning Herald*, it is constructed in terms of the public. So the former focuses on an individual, 'Norm', (the Union's general secretary) who 'is too busy'. Much of the article uses direct or indirect quotations of Mr Gallagher's words (or rather presents these as quotations — they may not be that). Consequently the voice of an individual dominates this report; the Union is represented through

Full Bench announces decision on BLF today

By MATTHEW MOORE,
Industrial Reporter

MELBOURNE: A Full Bench of the Arbitration Commission will this morning bring down its decision in the deregistration case against the Builders Labourers' Federation.

The three-member Bench, headed by Justice Terry Ludeke, will hand down its decision at 10 am, just two weeks after it finished hearing evidence in the case, which began seven months ago.

It is considered almost certain that the decision will grant the Federal Government its application, enabling it to deregister the union federally.

A large police contingent is certain to be on hand in case of any demonstration by BLF members, although the union's general secretary, Mr Norm Gallagher, said no security would be necessary as no demonstration was planned.

"They're too busy working and getting the 3.8 [per cent]," he said, maintaining his claim that BLF members have not been disadvantaged by the commission's refusal to pass on last November's national wage increase.

Mr Gallagher said no officials would be present although the BLF's legal advisers would attend.

"Why should I go?" he said. "I've got work to do. I have had these decisions before. This thing has been going on longer than *Blue Hills*."

If the Federal Government gets its decision as expected, it will then be able to cancel the union's Federal registration, which will trigger Victorian legislation cancelling the registration in Mr Gallagher's home State.

The BLF has already been deregistered as a State organisation in NSW.

Until the Federal Government acts, the BLF will remain a registered body and the complicated business of trying to carve up the union and distribute its members to other unions will not get under way.

The Victorian Government has already released a draft plan for breaking up the union and it is believed the Federal Government has virtually finalised its own actions.

A report in a 'public' mode from the Sydney Morning Herald

Too busy for court, says Norm

NORM Gallagher will not attend an Arbitration Commission sitting today to hear its decision in the deregistation case against his union.

"I've got work to do," the general secretary of the Builders Labourers Federation said last night.

Nor will BLF members demonstrate opposition to the proceedings.

Mr Gallagher said: "They're too busy working and getting the 3.8 (per cent national pay rise)."

He maintained his claim that BLF members were not disadvantaged by the commission's refusal to pass on last November's national wage increase.

Mr Gallagher said he did not know whether the commission would declare, as the Federal Government wants, that his union breached its undertakings and commitments to the centralised wage-fixing system.

He said: "I've had these decisions before."

A spokesman for the Victorian Employment and Industrial Affairs Minister, Mr Crabb, was confident yesterday that the commission would declare that the BLF breached undertakings and its commitments to the national wage-fixing principles.

He said this would lead to a chain of events which would mean deregistration and ultimate dismantling of the union.

Mr Gallagher . . . no time to hear decision

A report in a 'private' mode from the Daily Telegraph

the voice of its individualised leader. The concerns expressed by 'Norm' are the everyday, commonsense concerns that readers of the *Daily Telegraph* might be expected to accept as concerns of unionists, or perhaps to understand in terms of their own experience. The *Sydney Morning Herald* on the other hand places the event into the domain of the public. The focus is firmly on institutions: 'a full bench of the Arbitration Commission', 'The Builders Labourers Federation', 'the Federal Government'; and the focus is also on institutional action presented in the nominalised, objectified form that I pointed out in the Minister's letter: 'its decision', 'the deregistration case', 'its application'. Agency lies with these abstractions, so that 'the Arbitration Commission' — rather than the judges (or the presiding judge) — 'brings down its decision'; and it is 'the decision' — rather than the judges — which 'will grant the Federal government its application'.

As one final example of this process at work, here is an interview from the evening news on Sydney's Channel 7, a commercial television station. The occasion was the return of Mr John Howard to Sydney after a series of extraordinary events in the preceding week had led to his election as leader of the federal opposition.

ROSS SYMONDS: Now/back to today's main news story/Opposition leader John Howard/. . . he's just flown in at Sydney airport/. . . back from a tumultuous week	TALKING HEAD
5 in Canberra/and home for the first time as party leader/but before he drives home/Mr Howard has agreed to talk to us live/tonight/well	L.H.S. pic of SYMONDS WITH NAME UNDERNEATH.
congratulations John/and welcome back	R.H.S. Howard with name
10 to Sydney	and *Seven Nat. News*
JOHN HOWARD: Thanks/Ross/and it's	and *LIVE* above both.
nice to be home/(extended pause)	C.U. of Howard in car.
R.S.: Well/tell me/ . . .ah/ . . .you've had . . . uh/ . . . what/ . . . one day of your	
15 planned week skiing with your family/ there's no more holiday in sight/your wife and children must be pretty cranky	
with you/huh?/	John Howard + liberal
J.H.: They are/they've really learned	party logo at bottom.
20 the truth of the adage/that a week is a long time in politics/in fact/Thursday demonstrated that/. . . a day is/. . . (blurred) so/. . . it's been one of those very very	

tumultuous weeks in existence/but I'm . . .
25 very very lucky that Janette and the kids/
have sort of helped and understood
R.S.: How are you feeling now/after the   Cut to side-by-side
last few days?/   shot.
J.H.: Well/obviously I'm still   Howard in car.
30 very honoured and elated/that the party
should have asked me to be its leader/
it's been a bewildering sequence of events/
but I've got ahead of me/on the weekend/
so much work to do/that there's not a
35 great deal of time/to . . . luxuriate/ . . . in
the exhilaration of it/but/ . . . I really am
very honoured and privileged/that the party
should ask me to be its leader/
R.S.: You probably noticed a headline this   TALKING HEAD
40 morning/John/which describes you as
the man Labor fears most/ . . . how do your
children react to that sort of thing?/   Howard in car.
Do they see you as some sort of political   name + *Liberal Leader*
ogre/ . . . (under H.'s reply: or just an ogre?)
45 J.H.: Well/I think my eleven year old
daughter/is starting to understand what it's
all about/but the boys of 7 / 5 / and 4/
they're aware/that something's happening/
but the consciousness of it/is not
50 really sinking in/but I must say/in
political terms/I'm flattered to note/
that Mr Hawke is already violently attacking
me/that's a good sign/
R.S.: Well/getting back to real   side-by-side shot.
55 politics/ . . . Mr Hawke is obviously your
personal target/What do you think are his
two main weaknesses?/
J.H.: Oh/he's/ . . . uh . . . he's/ . . .uh. . .   Howard in car.
he's extraordinarily sensitive to personal
60 criticism/and when it really comes to
the crunch/ . . . he walks away from tough
decisions/the MX missile . . . uh/ . . . remains
a monument to his failure/to hold his
nerve in the national interest/when a
65 really tough decision is required/up
until then/I was actually saying comp-
limentary things/about Mr Hawke's foreign
policy/he largely continued the support

of the American alliance of the Fraser
70 government/and previous Australian govern-
ments/but he really gave the game away on
that issue/and I don't think/he's ever been
the same man on political issues since/
R.S.: So/you don't think he's a
75 formidable opponent at all?/
J.H.: Oh/ . . . I never take opponents
lightly/but he's certainly not that un-
beatable/charismatic strong-man/that
many Australian's thought he was/in 1983-84.
80 R.S.: Well/John/you're known to like   side-by-side shot.
a party like the rest of us/what are you
planning for tonight/kick your heels up?/   John Howard in car.
J.H.: Well/no/very quiet night
tonight/I think/ . . . we're all a bit tired/. . .
85 but the family . . . /but tomorrow night/we're
just going to have a few friends and the
family over/for a few drinks/ . . . but/uh . . .
tonight's going to be/a very quiet night
with the family/
90 R.S.: Well/thanks for joining us   side-by-side shot.
live tonight/John/and all the best
for the future/
J.H.: Thanks a lot Ross/

One might expect that this interview would be concerned with some
exploration of the issues that had led to Mr Howard's election, perhaps
a discussion of new directions to be pursued, differences in policy, difficulties within the party. But there is none of that. The direction of the
interview is set pretty decisively from line 16, 'your wife and children
must be pretty cranky with you/huh?/', and continues in that vein — for
instance, line 41 on 'how do your children react to that sort of thing?/Do
they see you as some sort of political ogre/'. Even when the interviewer
is 'getting back to real politics' (lines 54-55) it is a matter of constructing
a debate around personalities, 'Mr Hawke is obviously your *personal* target' (my italics). The use of first names by the interviewer is an aid in
making this a personal matter. The leader of the opposition is clearly not
entirely comfortable with this strategy, and attempts to bring the discussion back to political issues (lines 62-71).

The tactics employed by the television announcer/interviewer are
remarkably similar to that of the *Daily Telegraph*. The interviewer has
the advantage of having the private medium of speech available as a fundamental aid; the newspaper has to strive to make the public medium of

writing more speechlike — hence its use of direct or indirect quotations in order to give the appearance of the dominance of speech. In other words, the forms of speech are imported into the written form. Something quite similar happens in this interview, though in the opposite direction. Mr Howard's language, is, in many of its formal features, much closer to the forms of writing. Constructions such as 'a bewildering sequence of events' (line 32), 'the exhilaration of it' (line 36), 'the consciousness of it' (line 49), 'extraordinarily sensitive to personal criticism' (lines 59-60), 'a monument to his failure' (line 63), 'a really tough decision' (line 65), are more characteristic of the written mode than the spoken. Furthermore, Mr Howard tends to speak in structures that are syntactically much closer to sentences than to simple conjoined clauses. Although I have not marked sentences in the transcript, a very telling difference exists between the structure of his speech and the structure of the woman speaker's. In her speech sense-units are nearly always the same as simple clauses: '/Whether they will come/or whether they won't come/or when they're ready to come/I don't know/... 'spose they'll notify us/but we've had/... oh/ ... had letters from them/...' That indicates that the basic pattern of her speech is formed by the equation of sense-unit = simple clause. In Mr Howard's speech that is not so clearly the case, if at all: '... he walks away from tough decisions/the MX missile ... uh/ ... remains a monument to his failure/to hold his nerve in the national interest/when a really tough decision is required/up until then ...'. Here at least three out of the six sense-units (or possibly four out of six) are not simple clauses (depending on whether we treat 'to hold his nerve in the national interest' as a simple clause). This shows that there is a 'mismatching' between syntactic structure (that of the sentence, the public mode) and the sense organisation (that of sense-units, the private mode). If syntax is thought of as more basic we can say that the woman speaker is basically attuned to the private mode, and Mr Howard is basically attuned to the public mode. The television station, because of its own political/ideological aims is forcing Mr Howard to act in tension with his basic orientation.

Social Occasions and Kinds of Text

I said earlier that text and social occasion are always inextricably intertwined, and much of what I have described so far has been an attempt to show just that. However, in my analysis so far I have not attended to the differences between these various occasions, their structures and processes, and so have not attended either to the differences between various kinds of texts. Up to this point I have discussed three interviews, two newspaper articles, the front page of a community newspaper, and an official letter. Clearly, the social relations coded in these various texts are very different indeed, as are the texts in their form.

Even the three interviews differ markedly; one could range them, for instance, in terms of the power differences between interviewer and interviewee, by the degree of control exercised by the interviewer. That might give an ordering where the university admission interview was top of the list in terms of power difference and control, the television interview second, and the interview with the woman last. In fact, there is a much greater similarity between texts one and two than between either of those and the last; so much so that it might be best to treat the last one as a different kind of text entirely. Whereas in texts one and two the interviewer exercises a notable degree of control and direction in the interview, in the last one the interviewer seems content to act merely as a prompter in order to get the woman to reminisce.

The difference could be characterised in these terms. In texts one and two the interviewer has a very clear purpose in mind, which is related to and derives from the institution in which he (in this case) works. He attempts to ensure that this institutionally derived purpose is achieved. In this he enlists the co-operation of the interviewee, though he is entirely prepared to be quite directive. The interviewees, for their part, have particular goals that they attempt to achieve (gaining admission to a university in one case; gaining public exposure and access in the other). There is a fair measure of agreement, a coincidence, between the aims of interviewer and interviewee. In the third case, the purposes are less clear, and less institutionally given. The interviewer had an interest in the area, the dam project, the views of local residents, and oral history. The interviewee's interests here are even harder to establish, perhaps they are the culturally widespread need for and pleasure in telling a story, in reminiscing, pleasure in narrative and in narration.

The very different form of the texts can be seen to relate to these social factors. This explains why the last of the three is not, in its form, really an interview at all — in its form it is one kind of oral narrative. The other two texts on the other hand show all the features of interviews: clear and controlled structures, clearly assigned roles (including speech roles), control of the topic by the interviewer. In other words, the formal structure of texts is closely related to the formal structures of social occasions. Given that there are recognisable and distinct social occasions in any one culture, it follows that there are recognisable and distinct kinds of text also. These recognisable kinds of text I will call — following a well-established tradition — genres. Genre is originally a French word meaning 'kind'; over a long period it has, in English as in other languages, developed a specialist meaning as 'kind of text'. Its traditional use has been in literary criticism, where it has been used to describe kinds of literary texts: novels, sonnets, short stories, epics, novellas and so on. More recently, the term has been used in film theory where kinds of films have been described and analysed — western, detective, musical, documentary, but also spaghetti western, psycho-western, Vietnam western, and so on.

My use of the term connects with these other uses, though my particular interest is in showing how texts are socially formed, so that I am perhaps somewhat less interested in all the formal aspects of a genre as such, than as signs rather of the social origin and nature of generic form. I am therefore not only interested in seeing *how* the front page of the *Daily Telegraph* differs from that of the *Newtown Voice*, but also in the details of *why* it differs in the ways that it does. My answer would focus on the political, economic, ideological place of both newspapers, the production processes, the social histories and present place of the producers, their view of their audience, the audiences' social make-up, their use of one newspaper or the other, their training as readers as well as the producers' training as writers and so on. Those questions would lead me to ask, in particular, how a specific genre positions me, or how the producers of a newspaper — whether commercial or community — attempt to position me as a reader, what kind of social person their text is instructing me to be.

In part I have already given some answers. The BLF article in the *Sydney Morning Herald* addresses me as someone knowledgeable about and interested in the processes of the state, in industrial legislation and machinery, and it treats me as someone who understands that the processes at work are abstract processes involving institutions and institutional relations. In making these assumptions about me, the writer of the article constructs a text that embodies all these presuppositions about me, and in doing so invites me (instructs me? coerces me?) to be the kind of reader envisaged by the producer of the text. *The Daily Telegraph* article addresses me as reader very differently. It assumes my understanding that these are matters involving wilful, powerful individuals — bosses, unionists, judges and politicians — whose concerns are much like mine, based on commonsense and experiences also much like mine. Again, in writing this article these assumptions shape the text this writer produces. However, both texts are public genres: they occur in that section of the newspaper that deals with political, public issues. Generically, therefore, I am constructed as a reader interested in the affairs of the public domain, as a public person. So in one case (the S.M.H.) the way the genre itself positions me and the way in which the text addresses me are closely aligned; in the other instance (the D.T.) they are not — unless I, as reader, accept that the public world really has this appearance, namely that of my own private domain. This is a mismatching which I personally find impossible to accept, and misleading. However, perhaps that demonstrates nothing much more than I am not an appropriate reader for the *Daily Telegraph*.

The main point is that every genre positions those who participate in a text of that kind: as interviewer or interviewee, as listener or storyteller, as a reader or a writer, as a person interested in political matters, as someone to be instructed or as someone who instructs; each of these positionings implies different possibilities for response and for action. Each written text provides a 'reading position' for readers, a position constructed by the writer for the 'ideal reader' of the text. I have given some description of that in relation to the two newspaper articles. As another example, take the letter from the Minister for Natural Resources. I showed how the Minister's position shifts from the *I* to the collectivity of *the government*, to quite vague, ambiguous or opaque positions ('broad based considerations' etc). In this the writer also positions the reader: as an individually conceived addressee — '*your* further letter', 'I share *your* concern'; as a member of 'the public' — 'Economic, social and environmental impacts must be examined. . .', 'a reliable source . . . to the people and industry of the lower Hunter'; or as someone who is knowledgeable about and interested in technical detail (from sections not quoted above) — 'Tillegra Dam in its ultimate development will supplement the existing major sources . . . It will supply a major part of the domestic, industrial and commercial water in the five Local Government areas . . .' This vacillation in the positioning of the reader is understandable given the likely mode of writing of the letter (put together by one or more public servants from bits and pieces of information already available, and given a little 'personal touch'). It is also offputting and distracting to the reader; he or she can't know how to respond to this letter, whether as individual, concerned citizen, or alienated by the bureaucratic mode of dealing with the question at such remove.

The ability of the writer to affect the reader clearly has the potential for ideological and political power. Much has been written about the effects of popular culture writing, of pulp fiction for instance, of soapies and other television dramas and serials, of quiz shows, and how they attempt to position and construct their readers and viewers. Advertisements are sharply focused examples of the attempt to construct and pos-

ition particular kinds of readers. Here is the text of an advertisement for
a moisturiser.

It doesn't take much to dry out your
skin. Working in an air-conditioned office
day to day or just working up a tan.
The solution seems simple enough.
5   Apply a moisturiser.
Problem is, once skin cells have dried
out, they have trouble absorbing and
retaining moisture.
All the water in the world won't make
10   them new again.
WE'VE TAKEN THE PERFECT ENVIRONMENT
FOR YOUR SKIN AND PUT IT IN A BOTTLE.
Vitamin E Skin Repair is not just a very
effective moisturiser.
15   Because it's rich in Vitamin E, it actually
helps repair skin damage so your cells can
re-absorb the moisture they've lost.
The result is healthy skin that feels
softer, smoother and stays that way.
20   Long after an ordinary moisturiser
would have left it for dead.
BEFORE YOU SOAK UP ANOTHER DAY'S SUN . . .
Let one fact sink in.
Your skin is your body's largest organ.
25   Yet, left to the mercy of our harsh
Australian climate, the outer layers will simply
die of thirst.
Before you take the plunge with just
any moisturiser, make sure you
30   choose the one that helps save
your skin as well.
Fast-penetrating, non-
greasy Rosken Vitamin E
Skin Repair.
35   You can lead your
skin to water.
We can make it drink.
FROM ROSKEN.
THE SKIN SPECIALISTS.

In the advertisement, spread over two pages of the magazine this text
appears on the right hand side, printed over an underwater picture of a
naked woman floating above a coral reef, with her back towards and just

above the coral. Above her body are the words 'This girl has dry skin'. Notice how the reader is written into this text. The reader is directly addressed as *you* ('your skin', 'your cells', 'your body', 'you take the plunge'), from the first line. But the reader is also written in in a host of other forms: 'Working in an air-conditioned office' where it is *you*, the reader, who is working; 'the solution seems simple enough' (seems to *you*); '*Apply a moisturiser*' (*you* are instructed to, or *you* will apply a moisturiser). However, there is also a second strand in this text, in which you and your skin, your body, your cells are prised apart, so that you begin to feel alienated from your own skin which now seems like some worrying extraneous problem. The lines I'm thinking about are, for instance, line 6 'once skin cells have dried out', where 'skin cells' can be read as '*your* skin cells', but can also be read as somehow existing independently, separately. Similarly in 'skin damage' (line 16); and also in lines 16-17, 'Your cells can re-absorb the moisture they've lost', where the cells are portrayed as acting independently, under their own agency. There are many other examples of this second strand, the effect of which seems to be to put the reader into a problematic relation viz-a-viz her skin, which now seems some alien thing with a life (or death) of its own. The resolution of this intolerable problem comes in the last line 'You can lead your skin to water. We can make it drink'. You, the reader, having lost control over your skin must place it (and yourself) in the power of the moisturiser.

The strategy of the advertisement to construct and position readers (as potential consumers) via a vast range of devices can serve as an example of the powerful effects of generic form, and its construction of readers and reader positions. Of course, no matter how prickly my skin may feel on reading this advertisement, I do not have to rush out and buy Brand X. I can refuse to permit myself to be positioned as the ideal reader of the advertisement, as of other texts. Though it is also important to point out that there are situations where this can be very difficult. Children in school refuse to be ideal readers at considerable cost — namely failure in the education system. Workers at their place of employment are often in similar positions; and anyone wishing to assemble their own bookshelf or install their own air-conditioning from a set of instructions would be foolish not to allow her or himself to be positioned by the text.

Institutions and Ways of Talking

It is at once obvious and puzzling why we don't all talk or write in the same way (leaving aside things such as voice quality). It is obvious when we consider the interconnectedness, the at-oneness, of language and other social matters. For if society is constituted of a variety of groups, separated or distinguished by class, age, gender, ethnicity, kinds of work, leisure activities, religion and political allegiance, and if texts are always formed in specific contexts with their complex meanings, then we ought to expect great differences in language use. Yet it is puzzling; for if we share in a common society, its values and its language, then why do we talk about 'the same' issues in such different ways? And why do people talk about such widely differing issues?

My answer agrees on the one hand with the proposition that we 'share' (whatever that may or can mean) in a common set of social structures and processes, and that we share in a common language, at one level of generality. We have to accept some commonality for otherwise it is impossible to explain why we understand each other at all. At more specific and particular levels however, the differences become more significant — and here our institutional affiliations are what really matter. What comes into play here are questions such as: What work do you do? What gender are you? How old are you? What is your ethnic background? What is your class affiliation, and — not the same thing — What do you think it is? What kind of education have you had? What sort of family background do you come from? The answers to these questions will give us important pointers to the kinds of things anyone is likely to talk about, and perhaps more important still, how that person will talk about them. I have already tried to give small indications of this: the way the elderly woman from a rural community sees the problem of a dam being built is very different from the way the Minister for Natural Resources sees it; and the way each talks or writes about that differs enormously. The elderly woman is as much formed by her social and linguistic history and present position as is the Minister; and those histories and positions are bound to differ in significant ways.

Meanings are made in and by institutions, in their everyday practices, in the way they mythologise about themselves, and in their constant interactions with other institutions. Take as examples the institutions of medicine, the factory floor, education and the law. Each has its own view of the world, which in many things reaches beyond the immediate concerns of either law or medicine or education. Each has its specific practices, its classificatory systems of relevant categories (illnesses, treatments, prescriptions, for instance) and all the linguistic technology that goes with these. The path of an individual from a particular type of family (with *its* notions of authority, gender-roles, political views, personal mores and values, social attitudes, and the uses of language that accompany these), to schools of a certain kind (with their values and practices, and the values and practices of a whole range of peers), into adulthood and into one of these institutions will leave her or him both socially formed and yet in significant ways different to others. So when a person with his or her specific history, social and linguistic formation, comes into an institution such as medicine, she or he will learn new meanings, new sets of practices and new modes of talking, which will come together with the modes of talking already learned and which have perhaps already become a part of that person. There will always be some tension in this: we all know professional people who have taken on the characteristics of their profession to such an extent as to have become entire stereotypes; and yet others do not fit so neatly into the mould. That tension can lead to new meanings, new combinations of forms from the person's prior experiences.

In the formation of any text, whether spoken or written, all these meanings come into play, often complementary, and, equally often, contradictory. In the text an attempt has to be made to reconcile these meanings. A good text is one that seems entirely natural, seamless, plausible. In a dialogue, a conversation for instance, there is a constant movement from the emergence (or raising) of a point of difference of meaning to the actual or apparent resolution of that difference. Here is part of a very much longer conversation among eight young people, most of them tertiary students. The social occasion is a meeting of friends and acquaintances at the home of several of the participants; the genre is that of conversation, a genre without formalised coding of power-differences:

	LIZ:	Yeah/Video type stuff.
	JAMES:	The next Gillian Armstrong
	LIZ:	Sound/yeah/just sound/ . . . walking round the
		street like we did the other day/for the rest
5		of my life/gee/that'd be fun/wouldn't it?
	JAMES:	The sound of bouncing cans
	LIZ:	Yeah/that's what we were doing the other day
		(inaudible)
	NEIL:	Sound effects
10		(inaudible)
	LIZ:	I'd like to do advertising/but you can't do
		everything in this course
		(inaudible)
	JULIA:	Advertising is ignored by all the socialists
15	RIK:	Is advertising sort of looked down on/is it?
	LIZ:	Well/everyone who does advertising/cause everyone
		does this course/to do sound and image type things
	PETER:	I think advertising sucks

	JAMES:	It's not that/it's that advertising is looked
20		upon as being very capitalist/bourgeoisie/
		whereas all the lecturers . . .
	LIZ:	bourgeois . . .
	JAMES:	whereas all the lecturers/are extreme left
		wing/so they really put it down
25	RIK:	I'm glad I don't have to put up with that sort of
		shit/in my course
	JAMES:	Yeah . . .
	LIZ:	We have a ball/we had a discussion on drinking
		coke
30	JAMES:	Depends on how you rate/how high you rate money
	LIZ:	. . . was supplying the capitalist economy/and
		oohh . . .
	RIK:	Oh no!
	KIM:	So what/Lay back and enjoy it
35	LIZ:	Yeah/why not?/If you don't buy it/someone
		else will
	KIM:	Exactly
	JULIA:	It's really fascinating though/what advertising
		does/how it invites you
40	LIZ:	Oh fascinating/I think . . .
	JULIA:	. . . positions you in the subject/and things
		like that/do you do things/do you/do do
		they consciously tell you/to put things here/
		and put things there/for a specific reason/
45		like to make a woman see herself in the model/
		and things like that?
	KIM:	Yeah/they consciously . . .
	SANDRA:	How can you think of it like that?
	LIZ:	But you'd have to/wouldn't you?
50	KIM:	. . . because it appeals to the people watching it/
		and they say/you're advertising a certain
		product/it has to appeal . . ./(unintelligible)
		. . . it feels wonderful
	LIZ:	Good ol's Sunlight/yeah
55	KIM:	. . . when you put it on/the woman is always there/
		sort of lathering herself/it appeals to the senses/
		that's all/so you have to think of that/in
		advertising/don't take it seriously/don't
		analyse it
60	LIZ:	In some countries they don't have advertising
	KIM:	Well that's a bit of drag/isn't it?
	LIZ:	But it gets to your subconscious/even if you say/
		I don't . . .

	JULIA:	But you're creating a world/if you look at it/
65		you're creating a world/that I don't know
		whether I would live in it/I don't know whether
		I could cope with the fact/that I was actually
		creating it/I mean I live in it now/but I
		think to myself/well/maybe I'll be able to
70		change it
	LIZ:	I'd like to do advertising
	JULIA:	It would be awful
	LIZ:	I'd like it
	JULIA:	. . . say/doing something you didn't like
75	NEIL:	But you're not going to change anything
	JULIA:	Why not?
	PETER:	Oh Neil/that's a terrible attitude
	NEIL:	Well/well you can't change anything
	JAMES:	We're learning to contribute to it/Neil
80	NEIL:	How/how?
	LIZ:	Well/often
	PETER:	What do you mean you can't/ . . . people are
		changing things all the time
	NEIL:	How?/How can you change things?
85	NODDY:	Like what?

The extract begins where one topic is being concluded, and another one ('doing advertising') is raised. I am particularly interested in two things: on the one hand, in how this text comes about as the result of differences, between individuals and their differing institutional histories and positions, and on the other hand, in how institutionally formed the meanings are which emerge here. The difference is between two views that I'll characterise as 'I'd like to do advertising' (line 11) and 'But you're creating a world . . .' (line 64). This passage of the text is constructed around that difference. I think it is fair to say that the views expressed by the members of the two parties are in no way novel, but are views that have wide currency in this culture. These views relate to particular institutional affiliations of more or less tangible kinds — such as social position, work (Kim, for instance, works in advertising), political affiliations, and so on. The views emerging here are not so much the views of particular individuals as larger scale institutional/social views of which these individuals are the bearers. (That might not be the view of the speakers; they would probably insist that 'That's just my opinion'.) As it is a conversation there is no strong pressure to find a real resolution of this difference, either by attempting to squash one view or by reaching a compromise. In a different genre, in a debate say, or in an argument, there would be such pressure, as there might also be in a high school essay. Here a superficially satisfactory resolution can be reached by agreeing to pursue a new topic which has emerged out of this present topic, namely the 'possibility of change'. So the prior topic and the differences about it are subsumed into this new topic. Agreement about topic change is a sufficient substitute for broader agreement.

Although there are the two dominant meanings around this single topic in this conversation, other meanings, other ways of talking do emerge, even if only marginally. There is the academic mode of talking (from line 39) '. . . how it invites you . . . positions you in the subject . . .' and the pragmatic professional's (lines 56-59) '. . . it appeals to the senses/that's all/. . . don't take it seriously/don't analyse it'; as well as hints of a way of talking that refers to notions of morality (lines 66-68) '. . . I don't know whether I could cope with the fact/that I was actually creating it'. These 'ways of talking' have been called 'discourses' and I will use that term from here on.

Spoken texts are always marked by such a multiplicity of voices — not simply the voices of individual speakers, but discourses, as the voices of social institutions speaking through or with the individual speaker. Dialogue, the multiplicity of voices, is the inevitable condition of all language use. That may seem an exaggerated claim. What about monologues? What about written texts? Surely it is obvious that they are produced by single speakers or writers. I would argue that what is true of conversation is true of all texts. If the meanings that we have, use, receive, argue over, impose, come from the institutions of which we have (had) experience, then given that we have all had experience of many institutions (family, education, bureaucracies, work, leisure, the mass media, religion, neighbourhood), the meanings available to us on any single issue are likely to be affected by a number of such institutions — however directly or indirectly — at first or second hand. For instance, while I am writing now I have in mind not only the various attitudes to language and social matters that have most immediately formed my own views (itself a dialogic process through my own history), but also the views I think some or many of the readers of this text will have. So my text now, as I write, is actually being formed by a dialogue between myself, various linguistic theories and their proponents, colleagues and friends with whom I now talk about such issues, and my imagined readers. While not all writers are perhaps always quite so self conscious, it seems to me that all writers act in precisely this way.

The writer's task is to produce texts in which the tensions between various discourses are always resolved, either by producing a text in which they are not (or barely) visible, or by clearly placing contending views in a hierarchy of valuation that strongly suggests to the reader how she or he is to read that text. One of the effects of popular culture may be precisely this: to deal with troublesome issues and to accommodate them in a text in such a way that the difficulties are resolved in particular ways. By saying this I do not wish to suggest that popular culture has no other uses; one major use is of course (this last qualification is itself a sign of a dialogue with imagined critics) in or for pleasure. Here are the opening pages of a Mills and Boon novel, *A Candle in the Dark*.

The Royal Heathside Hospital, in a fashionable
suburb of London, was the epitome of excellence in
modern medicine. Its structure of polished black
stone and gleaming chrome rose to an impressive
5   height of twelve storeys, contrasting sharply with
the small shops and streets of quiet Victorian
houses on its doorstep.
   At first there had been some protests when this
giant started to rise in the neighbourhood, but
10 during the ten years since its completion the locals
had grown proud of their new hospital. There were
700 beds in spacious and well-equipped wards and
the very latest technology in all supporting departments. Added to that, a thriving Medical School
15 and an efficient School of Nursing . . .
   'Why, it's almost a pleasure to be ill these days!'
So said Mr Lomond to Dr Stirling, the stalwart new
registrar, on his first visit to Addison Ward.
   The patient slipped his arm around the trim waist
20 of young Sister Bryony Clemence. 'They're a great
bunch of nurses on this ward, Doc, but she's the
cream!' He grinned at her embarrassment as she
eased herself away. 'You don't need to blush,
Sister.'
25   The houseman, John Dawson, accompanying Dr
Stirling, winked broadly at Bryony, but the reg
Istrar, concentrating on the charts he was studying,
either did not hear or chose to ignore the remarks.
   He glanced towards Mr Lomond, on Addison for the
30 control of his diabetes, and observed pleasant-
ly: 'Well, you seem to be stabilising nicely now.
You'll be going home before long.'
   The small group moved on towards their last
35 patient, but before discussion could begin both

doctors' bleeps sounded urgently. Making for the
nurses' station John Dawson picked up the telephone. After a brief exchange he came speeding
back to murmur urgently to the registrar: 'It's a
40   cardiac arrest, Simpson Ward'. Whereupon both
he and Grant Stirling were gone in a flash.
    Student Nurse Patty Newman, fresh from the
Introductory Block and full of enthusiasm, dogged
Bryony's footsteps. 'Does that mean we have to get
45   a bed ready, Sister?'
    Bryony smiled at her eagerness. 'No, the patient
will go to Intensive Care first . . . if they're in time'.
She adjusted a white hairclip holding the frilly
cap on her honey-blonde curls and glanced at her
50   watch as an orderly appeared pushing the patients'
tea-trolley. 'Well, I expect that's the end of rounds
for this afternoon. You can relieve Nurse Smith
while she goes to tea, Patty. She's in High Dependency, with Tina. You know, the new anorexic
55   girl.'
    The junior sped off to her appointed task while
Bryony detailed others of the staff to go to tea.
    The doctors' round had been later than usual that . . .

At first sight nothing particularly remarkable is going on here. It is
'simply' the opening of a popular novel, the scene-setting. But a surprising number of 'issues' emerge in these first two pages. There is, right at
the opening, the issue of development *vs* preservation, with the associated discourses of progress and environmentalism. These emerge in the
description of the hospital 'Its structure of polished black stone and
gleaming chrome' which 'rose to an impressive height of twelve storeys'
(3-5) which is contrasted 'sharply' with 'the small shops and streets of
quiet Victorian houses' (6-7). This is a 'fashionable suburb' so that we
can assume that (given its Victorian origin) it has undergone
'gentrification'. No wonder there had been 'some protests . . . in the
neighbourhood' (8-9). Nor is it quite likely that these protesters (professional middle class?) would be the kind of people who would have
'grown proud' of 'this giant'. That last comment seems to suggest this
writer's perception of how a lower-working class neighbourhood might
have responded: not knowing better initially, having to be told what is
good for them, and in the end seeing the wisdom of it all.
    There is also the issue of technology and progress in medicine, and the
quite fierce debates associated with that. This 'epitome of excellence'

with its 'impressive height' has 'spacious and well-equipped wards' and 'the very latest technology' (13). The doctors have their bleepers which can summon them to speed 'in a flash' to 'Intensive Care'. Notice how we as readers are positioned in such a way as to be entirely approving of medical technology; a phrase such as 'impressive height' suggests that we, the readers, concur with this judgment and are impressed. However, in among all the latest technology are some reassuringly old-fashioned touches: and perhaps none more so than the sexist attitude towards, and description of women. Mr Lomond, the elderly lecher, finds no difficulty at all in slipping 'his arm around the trim waist of young Sister Bryony Clemence' (19-20) who is 'the cream' of 'a great bunch of nurses'. Sister Bryony blushes obligingly, as she is meant to do in male fantasies of women, and later she adjusts 'a white hairclip holding the frilly cap on her honey-blonde curls' (48-49). The houseman also knows how to behave towards subordinate females, winking 'broadly at Bryony', indicating to her and to us that it is perfectly in order for her to be sexually harrassed by an elderly male patient.

The issue of the treatment of gender roles and gender relations, treated here in sexist discourse, is itself embedded in another discourse, that of authority and hierarchy. This is outlined in the carefully sketched work-role relations — *Sister* Bryony, *Nurse* Smith, *Student Nurse* Patty Newman — with clearly indicated authority relations. Bryony can order Patty 'You can relieve Nurse Smith, while she goes to tea, Patty' (53-54) and indeed can call her 'Patty', while Patty has to call Bryony 'Sister', and Bryony is careful to use Nurse Smith's title to Patty. The role relations between the male medical staff are equally carefully drawn in, as are the relations across the gender/status/professional line of doctor/nurse.

These discourses are interwoven with medical discourse itself. To give just a few examples. 'Mr Lomond, on Addison for the control of his diabetes' (29-30); here diabetes is treated as a possession, an integral part of the person, like 'his blood', 'his right leg'. 'You seem to be stabilising nicely now' (32) where the illness and the patient are conflated by being named as the same; rather than 'your diabetes is stabilising . . .' or 'the level of sugar in your blood is stabilising . . .' 'It's a cardiac arrest, Simpson Ward' (39-40); here too the name of the illness has become the name for the person, who has quite receded from view. The same is the case with 'the new anorexic girl' (54). Being 'new' she still has her name, though it is not hard to see that before long she too will have become 'the anorexic girl in High Dependency'. The nominalisations used here (nouns made from clauses describing actors, actions and effects) — *High Dependency, cardiac arrest, Intensive Care, the control of his diabetes* —

are not far removed in their effect and function from the forms used in the Minister's letter. Obviously very similar processes are going on here, processes of distancing, of objectifying, of creating a new world that can in part be controlled through the control of language.

Gender, Class and Language

More is going on in the Mills and Boon text, more is being communicated here than meets the eye. Among other things, sets of values, attitudes on specific issues are being communicated, as covert instructions to readers to think certain things, take certain kinds of stances, perhaps even to be a certain kind of person. Of course there is as always the possibility of rejecting the suggestions of this text; in this case there is no immediate coercive power at hand to exert its influence on the reader. Nevertheless, the instructions conveyed here are quite in tune with very many other texts: advertisements, short stories, conversations in the office, on the bus, at home, all sorts of light reading and entertainment. The message of this text is not an isolated one; it is constantly reiterated in many places. The fact that it is 'merely' reading for pleasure, 'just' a Mills and Boon romance may make its message more effective.

One of these instructions, coded in the sexist discourse, is about gender and gender-relations. Implicitly, it tells the largely female reader many things not only about how women, but about how men and women should be, and how they should interrelate. Some have to do with what jobs are appropriate for men and for women (professional for men, semi-professional for women), how men and women can or should interact (the arm around the waist, the knowing wink, the embarrassed blush), and about what is appropriate and acceptable behaviour. The text indicates that women are or should be interested in their appearance (the touch of the hairclip) and should cultivate a 'feminine' appearance ('the frilly cap' on the 'honey-blonde curls').

Messages about gender-specific behaviour are among the most insistent and widespread in our culture, and they tend to be coded in the most diverse forms of activity. Much has been written on this from the point of view of women's language. It is interesting to note straightaway that it is women's language and not men's that has tended to be the focus of attention. This reflects the fact that those with greater power have the right to make an object of study of those with lesser power, and to take their own behaviour as an unquestioned neutral starting point. This is as true of women's language as it has been of working-class language and of 'exotic languages' before that. I will attempt to focus on gender difference in language use, both of men and women.

In discussing gendered language a number of questions need to be addressed. How are men and women talked about? How have men and women learned/been taught to think of themselves? How do men talk and how do women talk? How do women talk to women, and to men? How do men talk to men, and to women? How is the relation of the sexes constructed in language? Obviously I will be able to do no more than throw out a few hints in these areas. The Mills and Boon romance gives an indication about how we might answer both the first and the second question. We would need to look at very many texts in a particular culture, describe who participates in them and in what roles, who writes them, who reads them and how, and try to assess what effects these texts have had. This would be no mere academic exercise. In public debates about the effects of television violence or the availability of pornographic materials that is precisely the question at issue. In those debates it is assumed that the continuous exposure to texts of a certain kind positions readers/viewers in particular ways toward violence, or sexual relations, and acts as a constantly insistent instruction to readers to accept such views and perhaps to see them as possible modes of being and acting.

The answers are likely to be not at all clear and certainly quite complex, though my own theoretical position suggests that texts do indeed have that tendency. Here I will discuss two texts that permit me to ask some of these questions, and to indicate how we might begin to get answers, and what those answers might be. Both are brief interviews; the interviewer is the same in both. The interviews were conducted in order to get some materials for a radio program on language.

 Interview 1

  MAX: This is for a radio program that I'm doing John
     ah ... um ... Two questions that you can answer
     briefly the first is what would you say language
     is, what is language?
 5 *JOHN:* What is language?
  MAX: Yeah
  SID: Communication
  JOHN: Well it's a it's a it's a different form yeah it
     is communication
 10 *MAX:* Communication
  JOHN: What do you mean from different people from all
     over the world?
  MAX: Yeah
  JOHN: What would you say language is that? It's just
 15   ah haha Jesus Christ that's that's that's something
     you take for granted I don't know
  MAX: Yeah? What would you say it's made out of?

Interview 1

JOHN: Noises . . . different noises

MAX: Terrific thanks a lot

20 JOHN: I don't know it . . . it . . . it's a question . . .
            it's very hard to . . . what would *you* say language
            is?

SID: Well it's made out of . . .

JOHN: What what what is language?

25 JOHN: -ation

SID: Language is communication between people that . . .
            but language instigated bullshit that's where it all
            came from you couldn't talk there wouldn't be so
            much bullshit around it . . . it's between people of

30   a . . . it's a . . . communication between people

JOHN: Sounds, Yeah

MAX: That's wonderful thanks a lot

JOHN: Ha ha ha

SID: That's very interesting

Interview 2

MAX: A couple of questions very easy to answer for a
            radio program we're doing the first of the
            questions is: *What* would you say language is?

WOMAN: Language . . . well it's the dialogue that people

5   speak within various countries

MAX: Fair enough aaand *what* would say its made
            out of?

WOMAN: (8 second pause). It's made out of
            (puzzling intonation)

10 MAX: Hmm

WOMAN: Well I don't know how you'd tell what it's made
            out of it's a person's *expression* I suppose is it?

MAX: I haven't got the answers I've only got the
            questions (laughing)

15 WOMAN: (simultaneously — small laugh)

SID: That's not *bad* though

WOMAN: Well it's an *expression* it would be a person's
            expression wouldn't it?

SID: That's a good answer

20 MAX: Thank you very much

The context of the two interviews was that Max went to collect his car
which was being repaired at the garage of which Sid and John are joint
owners. After Max had finished his first interview, he turned to interview
an elderly woman who had driven up to get petrol for her car. This in

itself explains some of the differences — Max's familiarity with Sid and John, and his unfamiliarity with the woman had obvious effects on the two interviews.

Yet context alone leaves most questions unanswered. For instance, in their answers the men use the present tense 'Well it's a it's a it's a different form yeah it *is* communication' (8) or 'Language *is* communication' (26), which has the effect of making statements seem immediate, real, factual. The only exception is where Sid speculates on life without language '(if) you *could*n't talk there *would*n't *be* so much bullshit . . .' (28). The woman varies between the use of this present tense '. . . well it's the dialogue that people speak . . .' (4) and the apparently hypothetical form '. . . how you'*d* tell . . .' (11), '. . . it *would be* a person's expression . . .' (17). I say 'apparently hypothetical' because it seems to me she is not using it hypothetically in the normal sense, but rather in order to distance herself from what she is saying, and through that, from the interviewer. That seems borne out by the fact that the woman uses other distancing devices. In her first answer she uses the definite, factual *is*, but in subsequent answers she shifts to a form expressing doubt or uncertainty. So for instance, lines 11-12: '. . . it's a person's expression (certainty) I *suppose* (uncertainty/tentativeness) *is* it? (uncertainty/tentativeness)' or, again, line 17 'Well, it's an expression (certainty) it *would be* a person's expression (uncertainty/tentativeness), *would*n't it (uncertainty/tentativeness)'. The men make no such shifts. Why do men feel more confident about their answers? Do they value their knowledge more highly than the woman values hers? On the face of it it seems to be so. Of course, this has nothing to do with the actual status of the responses; after all, they are sought as 'opinion', and that is what they are. It may be that women have been taught that in interaction with men they should present their views in a tentative form, to undervalue the status of their knowledge. What we would need here are texts that are records of interactions between women; we might then see a difference.

Why is the second interview so much shorter? One reason is that the men talk much more than the woman. Another is that they are quite prepared to ignore and override the interviewer's control of this text. So for instance, in the first interview Max addresses his question to John, but Sid enters quite unbidden and offers his answer (7). When Max wants to close off the interview with 'Terrific thanks a lot' (19), John quite ignores that instruction and continues on 'I don't know it . . .' (20). Max's second attempt at closing the interview 'That's wonderful thanks a lot' (32) is still ignored by Sid. That certainly is not the case with the second interview. Max's 'Thank you very much' (20) is sufficient to close the inter-view. So there are differences here too: the men speak more, or perhaps, the woman speaks much less in the interaction with the male interviewer and the male 'bystander'; and furthermore, she is not willing or inter-ested in challenging the interviewer's control of the interview.

There are other differences. The woman does not swear; no 'Jesus Christ that that's something . . .', 'language instigated bullshit . . .' The interviewer addresses the man differently from the woman. To the men: '. . . radio program that *I'm* doing . . . Two questions that you can answer *briefly* . . .'; to the woman 'A couple of questions *very easy* to answer for a radio program that *we're* doing . . .' Why, we might ask, should the answer be presented as 'brief' for the men, and as 'very easy' for the woman? Is it simply that the male is busy at work? Perhaps the woman was in as great a hurry? Lastly, why does Sid feel it necessary to validate the woman's answers 'That's not bad though' (16) and 'That's a good answer' (19) when he seemed to see no need to do the same for John?

These two interviews can tell us some things about gender and language. Obviously we cannot base too much on two brief interactions, though my conclusions here are in broad agreement with the quite enor-mous amount of work that has been done already around these questions. And indeed there is an affinity between the way women are presented in *A Candle in the Dark*, and how the men relate to the woman and how she represents herself in the interview. My view is that the constant experi-ence of social occasions and particular kinds of language uses, the insist-ent experience and instruction of texts, can lead to the acceptance of particular views about oneself. Therefore it matters a lot what kinds of social occasions individuals have experience of and how they are pos-itioned in those encounters, what kinds of generic form anyone experi-ences and how they position readers, what kinds of institutions and discourses we encounter, and who and what they tell us to be.

The Mills and Boon novel constructs women and men in particular ways; it provides ways of talking about women and men, which, together with countless other texts, affect the way men and women come to see themselves, each other, and the possibilities of their interaction. The interviews show how such conceptions of gender can and do work out in interaction. The men talk in ways that are indicative of how they see themselves (at least in this situation) and their relation to the male inter-viewer. The woman talks in a way that is indicative of how she sees her-self (at least in this situation) and her relation to the interviewer. Max's formulations and Sid's comments also give some hints about their con-ception of the woman and how to interact with her. The language used registers these things in a finely nuanced way.

The social definition and valuation of the biological category of sex-gender has its particular articulation in each specific culture and period. My examples give some indication of how this might be working in one facet of Australian culture. Linguistically speaking, the expression of gender difference has much in common with the expression of differences of power that derive from other sources. For instance, the kinds of forms Brian Gentle uses to achieve distance and tentativeness are quite like the woman's in the interview. This might seem to suggest that gender is just one of a number of categories giving rise to power-difference. The letter from the (female) Minister for Natural Resources to the (female) addressee has many forms indicating power-difference. More than that, the language of the letter differs greatly from the language of the elderly woman. The difference here is perhaps best characterised as a difference of class. The fact that the two speaker/writers are of the same gender does not lead to sameness of language use. Class, or difference of class, seems to override the effects of gender on language use. In other words, gender is one determinant of language use, but only one. A question to be resolved is whether it is the major one, or one among several, or whether it is secondary to the primary determinant of class.

I have no conclusive answers, but will venture a hypothesis based on the texts I have discussed so far. Before I do so I need to say something about my use of the term 'class'. In the second chapter some of the main characteristics and determinants of class were indicated, and you may wish to refer back to the discussion there. 'Class' is one of the most problematic terms in sociological theories. In my use here I do not wish to put forward a particular view, other than to assert that in a society such as Australia's in this century matters such as the distribution of wealth, access to educational facilities, the professions, control of state institutions, have been such as to give rise to broadly differentiated groupings of the population, which I refer to as 'class'. Membership of a specific class brings with it particular orientations to power; that is, power is not equally accessible to all classes, and different classes have or exercise different kinds and degrees of power. My assumption is that the interests of the differing classes are not identical, indeed they may conflict with or contradict each other.

Given the very different social organisations of different classes, language is likely to reflect class difference through socially distinctive modes of speaking, ranging from differing 'accents' to different access to the linguistic resources of grammar. In interactions the differences of power between classes are unlikely to have their effect directly; for instance, someone with an upper-class accent cannot on that basis alone ask me to remove my rusting Holden to make room for his or her shining red BMW. Rather, class power is mediated through institutions: I am likely to find that a government minister or company executive has a specially designated parking space that I may not use. Or I am likely to find that the person with the red BMW is also the person who can offer me employment, do the operation on my hernia, or sign the letter that tells me that my house will be bulldozed to make room for the new freeway. So in my discussion from here on I will use 'class' as a shorthand term to describe the whole complex I have just indicated, and will assume that in interactions across class boundaries, and frequently within class, the interrelations of the participants are mediated through institutions.

In interactions where the speakers are of the same class and of different gender, gender tends to determine power. An example is the interview with the woman. Here the greater power rests with the men. They use more definite forms, speak more, direct the text more than the woman. Where the speakers are of the same class and gender (the 'admissions' interview), power differences derive from other factors such as age or status. In interactions where the speakers are of a different class and of the same gender (the example of the Minister's letter), power derives from class difference. Where the speakers are of a different class and gender the situation is slightly more complex, since both of the power variables are at issue. If the male speaker is of upper class, gender-derived male power conjoins with, and reinforces, class power. If the female speaker is of upper class, the two power variables are in contradiction: class power is with the female, gender-derived power is with the male. None of the texts I have discussed so far include that situation. From my observations women in those situations cannot automatically rely on class power (or status-derived power); indeed they tend to have to work hard and constantly in order to maintain equality, let alone superiority of power.

This is a complex picture. Moreover, it has a very different look for men and for women. Out of the five cases I have described there is only one where gender is an issue for males, the situation where the female interactant is of upper class. In the other four instances gender does not emerge as a problematic issue for men. In interaction with women, men are always advantaged by one of the two power variables. In interactions with other men, power derives from institutional sources such as class or status. For men, therefore, class/institutions seem to be the source of power; for men the picture is one in which gender doesn't matter because it doesn't even appear; it is to all intents and purposes invisible. It is a picture where men 'naturally' have power, except in the one 'unnatural' instance where the woman occupies a higher class/institutional position.

For women the picture looks entirely different. For them the picture is one where gender is nearly always — in four out of the five possibilities — a problem; gender is constantly visible. The picture is one where women 'naturally' have less power; and even where they have institutionally (or class) assigned power they have to struggle to assert it or to have it acknowledged. To all this we need to add the fact that for a very long time powerful institutions have been, and still largely continue to be, controlled by men. The experience of women is one where they hold few powerful institutional positions. In very simple terms, most women have men as their bosses, most men have men as their bosses, and very few men have women as their bosses. Men encounter institutional power most usually in the form of other men; whereas for women institutional power wears the face of the opposite sex.

So, for men gender is not an issue; power seems to derive from class and institutional power. For women gender is *the* issue; gender and class/institutional power appear as the same. My analysis leads me, therefore, to say that the male position is a particular ideological position, and is based on the need to preserve male power. However, I believe that the female position (as represented by me here) is also ideologically specific. My argument rests on the long cultural identification of male power with class power, which I see as an attempt to make the social (class power) seem natural (male power). That is, an argument has long existed which identified the social/cultural classifications and valuation of gender with the inevitable facts of biology. Thus cultural difference could be made to seem natural and therefore unquestionable. By linking and even identifying class power with male power, class-based power could come to seem natural too. And so by pressing gender difference into the service of class difference, as one ubiquitous expression and articulation of it, class difference could become invisible and natural, and could be replicated everywhere in authority relations that did not appear class based. Vesting institutional power everywhere in males has made gender invisible as an issue for those who hold power, and at the same time has made gender appear to be the dominant issue for those with lesser power. In my view gender is very much a problem, but it is a problem through its identification with class power. The prior fact of class power seems to me to be fundamental.

In this discussion it may seem that I have strayed a long way from

'Language, culture and communication', though I do not think so. I am attempting to answer two questions that seem most important to me. One is: why is it that the forms that characterise what has come to be called 'women's language' are so similar to the forms that characterise the speech of all those who have relatively less power in interactions? My answer is: on the one hand, gendered language is one instance of the effect of power difference on language, so that those are precisely the appropriate forms. On the other hand, if there were gender-specific forms of language (as there seem to be in many languages of the world), then the ideologically motivated identification of class and male gender in our society could not succeed. There would then be linguistic forms that indicated class-derived power, and linguistic forms that indicated gender-derived power. That would work to the detriment of those who have either or both kinds of power. My second question is: if this is correct, are we in fact playing into the hands of this particular ideological sleight of hand by continuing to focus on women's language? My answer is: yes, probably. It is a strategy likely to entrench the view for men that this is 'their problem', 'women's problem', when it is a problem for men and for women, a problem of economic and social structure at large. To me it would seem better to focus on the operations of power in language generally, including gendered structures of power and their appearance in linguistic form wherever they seem to be working to the detriment of any one group.

Language as a Mode of Social Action

In my discussion so far I have tried to describe some social and cultural institutions, some forms of language — mainly as kinds of text; I have analysed some of the interrelations of structures of power with some of the structures of language. At the same time I have tried to retain an emphasis on processes as well as on structures. In particular, I insisted on the importance of seeing all linguistic activity as dialogic, as always interactive. For that reason I used as examples quite a number of spoken texts of interactions. There is a danger in focusing too insistently on structures alone, for that leads one to see societies and cultures as static and immutable, entirely dominant and oppressive in relation to individual members of society, whose only possibility of action is acquiescence. Such a view is also entirely ahistorical, and so no account can be given of how the structures and the systems of value have come to be as they are, or how they might be changed.

Above all, if one is interested in going beyond analysis and descriptions to social action, then a view of language, culture and communication as process, as activity, as interaction, as always taking place in socially specific time, in history, is quite essential. And in such a view the individual participant in communication is significant — not as an individual in the traditional romantic sense of the unfettered spirit, but as both socially formed and socially agentive. Individuals are formed by and in their institutional and linguistic experiences and histories; in most or all encounters the meanings we encounter, produce, contest and reshape are socially, culturally and institutionally given. Yet they are encountered, contested and reshaped, imposed perhaps by individuals as social agents in communication.

The structures of power are ubiquitous, and may appear monolithic. And yet, as I attempted to show in my analysis of the admissions interview, or the 'Language instigated bullshit' interview, there is always the possibility of using such power as is available to the participants to *their* ends. The more awareness we have of the effects and meanings of linguistic form, the greater our possibility of using them for our purposes. At times it may suit our ends to acquiesce, at times it may suit us — and may be possible — to challenge a particular manifestation of power by using a subversive linguistic form. At times we may wish to mount a full attack on particular structures of power by an attempt to reform linguistic practices. This has certainly happened through the analyses of feminist critics who have had an effect on some practices of naming, as well as on other practices, for instance in the domain of legal changes, and in the domain of work.

In interactions the forms and structures of language are always 'at risk', open to challenge and change. Such challenges and changes range from the relatively trivial — such as contests over the pronunciation of a particular word — to the more openly significant, as in the definition of a word, the control of a metaphor, changes to a generic form — say, the writing of a science fiction novel which deeply challenges values about progress, control and about gender — or the reformation of modes of talking. At all times the institutional frameworks within which our communication takes place exert constraints. These may range from the constraints on teachers and their students in the education system, to the pressures experienced at work, or the more subtle effects of peer group pressures at home or at leisure. But in each case there are also possibilities of challenge. Teachers can ask questions about their own practices and the extent to which their language enforces and codes notions of authority and of what kinds of authority. Students can be made sensitive to the structures of power and of their interrelations and effects on definitions and conceptions of knowledge. This might lead to some realignment in relations of control and power, and would have effects on the structure of the curriculum.

The notion of language as social practice is one, therefore, that can lead beyond replication in our own lives of what is, and can lead us to challenge our own practices. While it is true that texts attempt to position us in particular kinds of roles and instruct us about what kinds of social persons we should be, it is possible as readers to resist these positionings and refuse the instructions. In all this I do not wish to put forward a merely anarchic view; my argument is not against order or hierarchy or control, all of which I see not only as necessary but as essential to social life. My argument is about kinds of order or hierarchy or control that are detrimental to those on whom they are imposed and probably in some ways to those who impose them.

As another very small example of changes in what I regard as the right direction, take the attempts to rewrite the official documents that affect people at large. The mystifying and alienating language of bureaucrats has been replaced by language that is more accessible, closer to the language of those who have to read, fill in or act on these documents. That has effectively meant that some power has been conceded by one group to another, though I would say with no ill-effects to those who have lost some power and with great benefit to those who have gained some.

At the same time I do not wish to slide into an unrealistically romantic notion of the powers of language or communication alone. Quite often in everyday discussions of communication near-magical powers are attributed to it. For instance, bad industrial relations may be attributed to 'problems in communication', and many a break-up of a relationship is blamed on 'breakdown of communication'. What is implied here is that if we can manage to fix up communication, 'get people talking to each other', everything will be well — bosses will get on with workers, and husbands and wives will find a new meaning in their marriage. That is naive. A greater awareness of language won't alter the problems posed by attempts to alter the distribution of wealth between shareholders, managers and workers in a company.

Throughout this chapter I have tried to stress the constant interconnectedness of language and culture/society. All linguistic action has social and cultural effects. There is therefore always a very real limit on how far linguistic action alone can go. Linguistic action alone will not reform society. Other kinds of social action will necessarily have to accompany the linguistic action. And there are always equally real limits to the extent to which the structures of power that anyone may wish to challenge can be challenged without provoking counteraction from those whose power is being challenged. Nevertheless, linguistic action *is* social action, and has real effects. Using linguistic forms that indicate certainty conveys to you the meaning that I am certain. However, were I to choose forms that might, at times, indicate tentativeness, it is not entirely unlikely that you might get some impression of a certain degree of hesitancy on my part. Certainty or hesitancy on my part will each call forth quite a different assessment and response from you, and so to that extent I have already altered the structures of the social relations in which we are both engaged.

I hope my discussion has given some new meanings to the notions that I wanted to challenge, namely that language is for communication, that language is transparent, that we all share a common language, that language is the neutral vehicle for the conveying of ideas, or that language is sounds and words and sentences. Language 'is for' or 'does' some of those things. But as I've tried to show, all of those notions have to be put into a much wider cultural and social context where they themselves take on quite new meaning, and where some of them have to be abandoned. Above all, I hope that I've succeeded in making that which may have seemed invisible quite noticeable, and that which seemed obvious and natural quite problematic. Language is a mode of social action, of acting in and on the world. It is for instructing, informing, for resistance and contestation. Above all, language is always *both* a means of control and a means of evading control and of effecting change.

Note

I wish to thank those students and colleagues on whose work I have drawn, wittingly or unwittingly, particularly Penny Fowler-Smith, Angela Georgiou, Sue Woolridge, Paul Alberts-Dezeeuw, Arnie Goldman, Stephen Muecke and Paula Hamilton.

Further Reading

Fowler, R *et al Language and Control* Routledge and Kegan Paul 1979

Halliday, M A K *Spoken and Written Language* Deakin University Press 1985

Kress, G R and Hodge, R I V *Language as Ideology* Routledge and Kegan Paul 1979

Kress, G R *Linguistic Processes in Sociocultural Practice* Deakin University Press 1985

Martin, J R *Factual Writing: Exploring and Challenging Social Reality* Deakin University Press 1985

Ponyton, C *Language and Gender: Making the Difference* Deakin University Press 1985

CHAPTER FIVE

V

Angles on the Image

by

Noel Sanders

Anthropologists tell us that members of cultures who are unused to photography have difficulty in understanding or deciphering, reading, photographic images. So even a photograph, which to us seems an entirely transparent image and 'merely' representational, is interpreted on the basis of cultural conventions. Without a knowledge of the codes involved in the construction of the photographic image we cannot perform the necessary semiotic work as viewers that would permit us to make sense of the image. Of course, when we look at the images of other cultures we immediately become aware that images are not transparent: they are highly conventionalised, highly constructed. Aboriginal Turingas do not declare their meaning to those who do not know the codes at issue.

In this chapter some of these conventions are laid bare, from the Renaissance invention of perspective to the use in current advertising practices of metaphoric or metonymic structures. Above all, the chapter insists that if we are unaware of how conventions operate in the construction of images, then we as viewer/readers are likely to slip readily into naive readings of images. Images are texts, similar in many ways to the structure of verbal texts. And just as verbal texts construct or provide reading positions, attempting to manoeuvre readers to adopt a stance suggested by the verbal text, so images as visual texts construct 'viewing positions', quite literally making a space for the viewer to take on. Without the viewer the image is incomplete, so that the effect is one where the viewer is pulled into an 'emphatic relation' with the image.

The chapter introduces the critically important notions of 'presence' and 'absence'. The terms are fundamental to the understanding of any cultural construct, and not just of images. In any text, whether visual, verbal, architectural, or a text of the code of dress and fashion, what is not stated, what is not there, is as significant as what is stated, what is there. The structure of presence/absence allows us to infer important meanings about the ideological constructedness of a text. Why does the text say what it says, why is it silent on this other point? What possibilities of reading are facilitated by this absence, or ruled out by that presence? Noel Sanders treats the visual image as a texture of cultural strands, a 'meeting place' and a 'clearing house of various cultural influences'. Like lace, it is a pattern of presences and absences; like the patterns of lace, the structures have cul-

tural origin and significance. And so the structure of the image is an ideological one, where cultural and social meanings, and the contingencies of the structures of the communicative situation exert their effect. Images are bearers of ideological meanings no less than verbal — or all other — texts, and readers/viewers are therefore positioned, and are participants, in complex cultural and ideological structures and processes.

Images

There is a series of usages of the word 'image' within society that carries with it the notion of falsity, contrivance and artifice. For a company to invent a corporate 'image' of itself is to present the public with what most would think of as 'PR'. There is something strange, for instance, about a Quiet Achiever that announces its quiet image with such force and ubiquity. To cultivate an image of oneself via clothes, haircut, mannerism and speech is usually taken as tantamount to putting on a disguise or adopting camouflage — the better to get on with what one's really on about. Image reaches its high point with the star or celebrity, that 'spectacular representation of a living being', who, as Guy Debord has written, 'embodies the image of a possible role. Being a star means specialising in the *seemingly lived*'.

Going to the dictionary for help can also be an illuminating experience. Until recent times, an image was a death mask that preserved the last 'living' expression of a corpse. More practically, the entymological meaning of image directs us to the final stage of emergence of an insect after all its previous stages from egg to larva to cocoon to, say, a butterfly, have been achieved. Gloriously fitted out in fine colours, the insect flies free, effacing all its less visually appealing stages, lives a day or two, then disappears to be replaced by others.

In religion, image usually turns up in the company of the qualifier 'graven' — the worship of which Christianity specifically refers to as being a dangerous affront to abstract faith. Other lexical unpackings of the word also play up artifice, and most hinge on image as a sort of crutch to visual perception, but a crutch that definitely endows the image with a life of its own, all the more powerful for the fact that its act of resembling comes about with the full recognition of its artifice.

In its turn, *artifice* in relation to Portuguese *feticao* (whence *fetish*), means *to fascinate*. A selection of definitions from the *Oxford English Dictionary* foregrounds this connection. Image can be an 'optical appearance or counterpart produced by light or other radiation from an object reflected in a mirror'. It can be a 'simile, metaphor or representation; an idea, conception, character of thing or person as perceptible to the public'. A mathematical definition of *imaginary* is something 'plotted perpendicularly to the axis of *real* quantities' — an idea that philosophy has recently taken up when referring to ideology as 'the imaginary (distorted, but specific) relocation' that the individual has to the real: that is, the bundle of beliefs, judgments, popular concepts, rumours and opinions that we use to construct reality.

In the following, I have made an attempt to pursue (in an entirely nonsystematic way) some of these leads, concentrating on the way that images in contemporary culture — whether from TV, magazines or photo albums — operate on and within society, especially with regard to the way that the viewer relates to them.

Depth and Surface in the Image

One of the most complex television events of recent times, the gigantic Rock Aid concerts in aid of the victims of the Ethiopian famine, presented viewers with extremes of visual fodder — from images of emaciated bodies to opulent food ads to performances by rock stars who have long set the pace for patterns of consumption in western society. The nameless poor and the names everyone knows, food in the survival sense of the word and foods known not through the substances that comprise them, but only by their prestige brand names — all were juxtaposed in seemingly violent contradiction.

For the viewer, what was involved was a similar set of major shifts in perspective — from close-ups of famine victims to longshots of the stars watched by their myriad fans; from unphotogenic refugee camps in Africa to the pleasure-domes of the great cities of the western world; from the multitude of the starving to the singularity of the starring. As well as these shifts in space and position of viewing, cultures and societies at totally different stages of development were juxtaposed in a way that is rare even for television. Yet despite these differences, the overall effect is the construction of a levelling, similarity and, in the end an 'identity', the basic humanness of us all: *We Are The World*.

In all this, despite the shifts in perspective required to take in all these shifts, we, the viewers, do not have to move an inch: through the perspective of television, close-up, zoom-in, pan, it all arrives, with its perspective pre-organised and pre-digested. The viewer's viewpoint has been constructed beforehand.

John Berger wrote in *Ways of Seeing*: 'Every image embodies a way of seeing'. It is possible to go a stage further and say 'every image contains instructions about how to view it'; or, further still, 'every image has a space within it that indicates where we are, not only outside the image but also within it'. A famous Sterling ad has disembodied hands entering the picture from the bottom right and left-hand corners of the image, implying that part of the viewer's body actually enters the frame. A Carlton beer ad features a table looking onto the sea, set for five; all seats are occupied, save one. This empty seat, the one nearest the bottom horizontal of the image is, the visual implication runs, ours. Similarly, a Coke ad has three people with the famous drink in their hands. Two are engrossed in each other and exchange smiles and glances; the third looks winsomely toward the view or inviting company and engages the viewer's wandering eye. Each of the images is, in a way, empty in just one aspect — incomplete in indicating the absence of the viewer, but at the same time inviting their presence, making the image complete.

The newsworthy famine images of Ethiopia, even though eventually capable of raising hundreds of millions of dollars in aid, nevertheless bear out the observation made in the 1930s by the German theorist Walter Benjamin (referring to photography):

> Photography is now incapable of photographing a tenement or a rubbish-heap without transfiguring it. Not to mention a river dam or an electric cable factory; in front of these, photography can only say: 'How beautiful' . . . It has succeeded in handling it in a modish, technically perfect way into an object of enjoyment (Walter Benjamin, pp. 94-5).

In 1985, faced with a 40 per cent penetration of video-recorders into the television market and with a declining clientele for live television (meaning, nowadays, television that is not recorded and in which ads are not zapped out), the advertising industry has produced the apotheosis of advertising — the ad for ads. The billboard image is a family seen at the far end of their (otherwise empty) lounge room. Their facial expressions are appropriately miserable, and the whole image is in black and white (usually reserved for 'prohibitive' ads like the 'Gangrene is one of the less glamorous aspects of smoking' and anti-drink/drive ads. 'There's one station these trains won't take you to' comparisons). On the surface, given the empty room and the deprived-looking faces, the scene denotes poverty and hunger, but the caption reads 'In some countries they don't have advertising to annoy them'. In effect, the caption captures the sympathy that wells up in the viewer on seeing an urgent image of deprived and hungry people and rechannels it into a plug for the super-rich advertising industry.

One of the ways this image works is by a construction of visual space, not least by putting the figures at a distance from the viewer, and leaving the foreground empty of detail. At the same time, the viewer's gaze is engaged by the family's eyes from afar, so that we must look into the background of an image where the foreground is vacant to get its meaning, causing the viewer to have the sort of vertigo that pulls them into an emphatic relation to the image.

In a way, the ad is a manipulation of the available equipment and techniques of image-decoding that viewers in this society would bring to such an image of 'deprivation'. Most contemporary images work on a convention of formal perspective invented in the Renaissance, albeit in a watered-down form. This convention relies most heavily on, as E.H. Gombrich wrote in 1961, 'a sense of depth combined with an unforeshortened portion of an object that appears to lie quite close to the frontal plane'. In a Gordon's gin ad, for instance, cocktail-hour gear is in such an unforeshortened position, near the bottom of the frame. Stretching away, a pool and then ocean drop away to a vanishing point.

Las Meniñas, *by Velazquez: the construction of the viewer's position*

What the foreground sees is a view; and what the viewer sees is presumably a vista brought to a peak of visual euphoria by Gordon's. In this way there is a sort of cause-and-effect relationship implied — the distinction between foreground and background is that of instrument to result. A further implication — conveyed by differing proportions of scale (that is, the relation of objects in the image to human size, form and proportions) — is that these bridgings involve the viewer.

The sense of *place*, then, in images, especially ad-images, comes not only from conventions of landscape, interior portrait or still-life representation (with whatever emphasis they might have on the visual and dramatic relationship of figures to backdrop), but also from the way the viewer is placed within or with respect to the image. If the image is in some way incomplete, indicating the viewer's place, then the image brings about its own particular form of closure or completeness of meaning only when the viewer's look is engaged — but engaged in a way prescribed by the image itself.

To elaborate some of these points a bit further, it could be useful to refer to a painting by Velazquez — *Las Meniñas* (1656) (figure 5.1). Here, the viewer's gaze is initially engaged by the small Infanta, and also by the tall figure looking directly from the left-hand side of the canvas. This figure is equipped with brushes and palette and is painting on a canvas on extreme left, the back of which is toward us. On first take, then, it may appear that the viewer is at the intersection of the two gazes — and that the painter may actually be painting someone outside the canvas as well as the child in the foreground. In a way the viewer is the subject of the painting as well as being the one who looks at it. But as the eye moves back in a narrowing spiral toward the back, what can be seen on the back wall is a square that can only be a mirror; and in it are 'reflected' two people, the proud parents, Philip IV of Spain and his wife Marianna. The viewer's position, then, is thus written into the painting in a very precise way. But at the same time, an elegant pun is being made on the way the viewer of the picture reads images in general, bringing about a contradiction between one's own look and that of the commissioners of the painting, the child's parents.

By way of contrast, consider one of the ads in the New South Wales anti-drink/drive campaign (figure 5.2). In the foreground here are two disembodied eyes, framed by a rear-vision mirror. In the background, in foreshortened perspective and out the back window of the car, is another car — a police car presumably in pursuit of the drunk driver. As with the Velasquez, the convention of the mirror both writes in the absence of the whole driver's body (with Velasquez only the parents' upper halves are

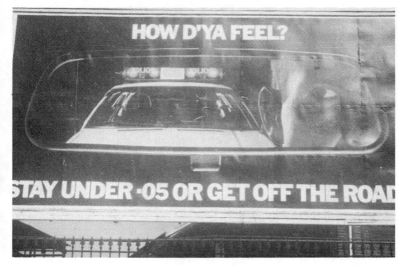

NSW anti-drink driving campaign

shown) and suggests the place outside the image where this whole
(viewer's) body is to be found. In both instances the placing of the viewer
is arrived at by the convention of mirrors. But these are only a few
aspects of the complex effect of relayed gazes. In each image there are
surfaces, constructing a feeling of depth by a succession of inlaid or
embedded surfaces that relay the viewer's gaze from the frontal surface
of the image back into the image, and then back out, to where, it is
implied, the viewer must be. Thus in the anti-drink/drive ad, the whole
image acts as a mirror, so that as one looks at the image, something in the
image (the police car) can be construed as approaching the viewer unseen
from behind his or her back.

Whilst these two instances may seem isolated they contain part of an
extensive repertoire of viewer-placing devices that run from traditional
perspective (with lines running diagonally away from the bottom/front
of the image to vanishing points at the back of the image) to empty spaces
in images to such trivial things as having tea-cup handles in ad images
pointing to the right (given that most people are supposed to be right-
handed). In most cases, the illusion of 'surface and depth' has the effect
of constructing relations of prominence (usually a foregrounded product)
that mediate between the viewer's position and some goal, reward or

vision in the background (hence the Gordon's ad). This bringing together of different things on the one surface is something perspective makes possible, unified under the singularity of the gaze of the viewer.

Image as Text

A common idea of what constitutes an image is of a static 'take' (a 'shot') of something in process. A 'still life' catches forms of vegetation or food with a negligence that (nevertheless) implies something before and after the image (the act of arranging flowers or preparing the food). A film-still, while apparently just one 'grab' from the film, also implies a narrative that both precedes and stretches away from the single image. Yet in both cases, while the image appears as a throwaway it still undertakes an essentialisation of the implied drama, process or narrative. And as such, every image implies a crucial moment of an action that both precedes and succeeds it. In this sense, the image's very urgency comes out of its appearance as climax, allowing the viewer to regard it as the key, or even keyhole, into some constructed reality.

While the word image may, as Roland Barthes has written, be close to its Latin source (*imitari*, to imitate), implying a frozen moment in which a match between reality and representation is achieved, it also implies that it is itself an action or process in which several ingredients come together and act dynamically within its frame. In this latter sense, the image comes close to the notion of text — that is, something that can be explained in itself, irrespective of what is narratively implied as coming before or after it.

The idea of 'reading' is something that usually goes with texts with a linear dimension to them (books, television, films). While still images seem to lack this time dimension, they have aspects of a more primitive notion of text. The word itself is derived from the Latin *texere*, to weave; and the idea that images weave together elements from different places leads to looking at them as a kind of mix of disparate elements that yet are presented together in a unified space.

In the advertisement for French Gauloise cigarettes, two different cultural geographies (one represented by the Eiffel Tower, the other by the Sydney Harbour Bridge) are 'mixed' together on the same surface. The presence of the painter in the ad implies he paints what he sees; but the image implies that he paints not what he sees but what he thinks. The effect is of a splicing of one reality onto another (or rather the superimposition of two realities) in a montage effect. The image is a weave not only of two different cultural geographies (French and Australian), but also of forms of representation, painting on the one hand, photographic on the other.

Images are texts, then, in the sense that we can read this difference on the basis of codes (of French-ness or Australian-ness) which, the ad-agency thinks, most viewers of the image will be able to operate. But they are also texts in the very primary sense of a 'weave' — as texture, or as textile itself. Anything woven is a fabric not only of presences (the fibres), but also of the spaces between. With lace, for example, the fabric is far more absence than presence, and any cloth is likewise going to be a combination of openness and closedness. Carrying the metaphor further, it is possible to take a written text as a combination of black, written elements and the white empty spaces of the page. The closedness of a newspaper text is to, say, nylon, as the openness of poetry (with its wide expanses of white paper) is to the open weave of lace or knitting. And like these latter text (-ures), both the Sydney Harbour Bridge and the Eiffel Tower are themselves texts, weavings of presences and absences — very open weaves in fact, being more not-there than there given their see-through architecture. As texts they incorporate spaces in their very make-up.

If the image itself is a meeting place or clearing house for diverse cultural references, as is the Gauloise ad, then it is possible to go one step further and look at it as being not just a text (a weave of presences and absences) but also as *intertext*. This concept was originally worked up by Julia Kristeva to designate the way in which one set of textual elements is transposed into (or superimposed onto) another. Out of this interleaving of two textual complexes (Eiffel Tower, Sydney Harbour Bridge, for example) comes a new one — perhaps even an ironical one. Roland Barthes, in *The Eiffel Tower* gives a detailed reading of that structure.

The genre of Australiana is a case in point. The repertoire of Australiana — koalas, Sydney Opera House and Harbour Bridge, Vegemite, Ayers Rock — operates on extremes of difference and uniqueness, backed up with a range of folklore, gossip, homespun talk, official and tourist texts. In each of the foregoing, an actual material, place or commodity takes on a connotation (Vegemite is vile and unsightly but indispensable and addictive and lovably unique; Ayers Rock is security, stability and centrality) that raises the object or place to the level of myth.

'As soon as there is society', wrote Barthes in *Elements of Semiology* (p. 47), 'every usage is converted into a sign of itself'. As soon as this happens, the object, place or commodity is well on the way to mythic status. In one sense, commodities 'as advertised' always aspire to this mythic level, not least by implying that buying them brings not only the use to which they can be put, but also a meaning that goes beyond this use. When, for instance, Stimorol chewing gum is advertised, it is said to be 'longer, stronger Stimorol . . . more than just chewing gum'. The implication of oral and sexual gratification unite in a meaning unspeakable in itself, but promised as a reward for buying the product. But precisely because this implication cannot be made 'literal' and speakable, it must be expressed at the level of an enigma that enlists the complicity of the viewer in a snide, nudge-nudge decoding of the meaning. The advertising of the product as 'more than just a chewing gum' goes right to the heart of what Karl Marx meant when he noted in the 1860s, that a product gets sold in the marketplace not just as a product, but also as a 'social hiero-glyph' — something not only to be consumed but also to be decoded. This is the point raised in Chapter Three, where Helen Wilson speaks of the Commodification of Information, and the industrialisation of culture.

While Stimorol elevates the product to the level of the mythic/sexual, products like MacDonald's elevate their products to the level of the mythic/national in television ads that make visual metaphors between Ayers Rock and hamburgers, and the Olgas and french-fries. Backed up and buoyed up by a range of popular myth, official and tourist literature (as well as other ads such as the building society United Permanent's insurance advertising, and Orthoxicol cough-mixture commercials), images of Ayers Rock come to circulate as signifiers of not just one con-cept, but of a whole host of concepts: Australian-ness, security, primevalness, scenic-ness, or whatever. In this respect, the Rock takes on the status of myth in two ways — not only in its status as the conveyor of notions of rock-like solidity and reliability, but also in the true role and function of myth itself: as a series of texts that can be read and re-read in all sorts of ways.

In its function as text, then, the image aspires to a bardic function, telling, re-telling and thus transforming the meanings that already adhere to objects according to particular generic or formulaic principles. When the Northern Territory Tourist Commission advertises the Rock as promising 'sessions' at various hours, it presents it in all the aspects we would expect of theatrical representation, taking in along the way all of the ready-knowns about the Rock and mixing them in with the promise of dramatic surprise. The Rock is strobed down into a succession of images, each lit in a way that implies the unfolding of a story, or even a sequence of stories or perhaps acts. Though these are implied only, they take up the spectacular aspect of the Rock as background for epic narra-tives such as the Azaria Chamberlain case, or smaller ones, such as the

United Permanent or Orthoxicol ads (both of which re-enact the beginning of the world and the formation of the continent with great geographical upheavals, in the space of thirty seconds apiece). In each instance, the Rock performs a narrative function in the sense that it carries with it all the imagery and popular mythology that surrounds it. In the sense that this visual text has a time element to it, in the more usual usage of text, it is one that is miniaturised and discontinuous, leading directly (especially on television) to a new one.

Paul Virilio, in his influential book *Pure War*, has maintained that we live in an age of *interruption*. On television, narratives such as soap operas are continually interrupted by ads; ads are interrupted by other ads. Given the fact that this technique of the media takes place in a time when nuclear annihilation threatens us all, the micro-narratives that make up ads fall under the overall possible scheme of The Great Interruption — the possible catastrophe that would wipe us all out. In such a world Virilio argues, what happens in the media is a series of micro-narratives that present, complicate and resolve scenarios and stories within very short spaces of time. The television ad is a classic case of this. Starting off with an enigma, problem, dilemma or fact, the television ad goes on to work this out with figures, situations and conditions, resolving the whole thing in favour of the product. When this rapid turnover of rusk-like mini-narratives becomes the mainstream of television, then we are in the era of 'picnolepsy' — a convulsive state you could say, of going from one image or image-narrative to another, breaking off from some narratives, breaking into others. (The word most like *picnolepsy* seems to be *epilepsy*, a physical state to which most of us, it seems, are susceptible, but which we mostly repress.) Picnolepsy, or the convulsion of the micro-narrative (video-clip or television ad) is what we are all into, it seems, to prevent the onslaught of realising the full import of The Great Interruption.

Alternatively, the micro-narrative may become a form of rehearsal that will allow us to experience interruption momentarily, and without the material loss that catastrophe in all its fullest meaning would imply. Already, Hollywood seems to have adapted to the concept of interruption — enough, for example, to have generated a number of films and television dramas that, on the one hand broach, and on the other (within the usual span of a movie) solve the problem of nuclear warfare or nuclear power catastrophe. (*The Day After* is an obvious example, but no less *The Never Ending Story* (albeit German) and several other features, realist or fantastic.)

For current purposes, however, we can note the effect that the micro-

narrativisation and symbolisation of a narrow range of nationally connected objects (The Rock, The Bridge) has. Visually stunning though
they may be in themselves, they lead to a view of society and culture that
is extraordinarily narrow — one in which whole histories, class and sexual differences are left totally out, in favour of a generalised address to
connotations of Australian-ness. Crystal clear though the images themselves are, their connotations are both unanalysed and (purposely)
unanalysable.

Family Snaps and the Image-Memory

In *Ways of Seeing*, John Berger proposed that the image is first of all a
'sight which has been recreated or reproduced'. The word 'sight' can itself
be taken in a number of ways. It is in some ways not just any visually perceptive act, but one that has been rigorously selected, either by finding
just the right 'sight' to take an image of (as in holiday photography) or by
a rigid procedure that selects from a multiplicity of shots (as in fashion
or advertising photography). In this sense, the image — and the photo in
particular — re-enacts an *act* of seeing.

A pun on the word 'sight' produces the word 'site' — and the image is
very much this, too. It marks a place where a meaning came together, and
where sets, objects and people assemble to produce a particular meaning.
In family snapshot photography, this 'siting' is almost literally the case.
You have to drop everything, arrange yourself within the group, adopt
the appropriate pose and get into the act of producing the family-snap-
meaning: the family as a coherent, happy unit whose continuity is
marked (sighted/sited) within a narrow range of 'observances' (birthdays,
weddings, Xmases). On these occasions, as in holiday snaps, the fact that
one is never snapped *doing* anything testifies to the contemporary function of the family — not as a productive unit, but as a leisure-time group
involved in consumption and the utilisation of 'free time'. Historically, as
Susan Sontag has observed, family photos came into vogue at precisely
the time in the late nineteenth century that the family was ceasing to
operate as a working, productive group and was being transformed into
a unit whose primary function was consumption. The relevant sites,
then, that family and holiday snaps choose as the space for forming their
meaning correspond to this actual shift in what the family actually *does*
— beaches, tourist attractions, restaurants, the lounge room.

Widespread use of photography is marked not only by its use by ama-
teurs such as family shutterbugs, but also by the institutions of the state,
such as the police, medical and educational institutions. The common
denomination is the role of photography in an overall process of surveil-

lance, whether it be police files, the documentation of mental illness, anthropological observation or the recording of bodily size or age under-taken by the family or educational institutions. Since the 1880s pho-tography has taken up a role that involves a shift from forms of knowledge based on reading or discussion to those based on the purely visual.

In all of these image-making practices, the individual is *placed* in some way — within the family, within school, within the law. This placing is, however, a particular structuring of the individual that has the effect of having them show up in very particular contexts. An example of this in Australia might be the practice in family photography amongst migrants of taking snaps not only of the family, but also of commodities acquired, for the purpose of circulating these images amongst family overseas. From this imaging of property, it is a small step to images as property, taking in along the way the display of family photos in living rooms and albums. For the family, as for the institutions of the state in general, photography performs an ideological function (an imaginary relation to reality, through the image) that John Berger takes in when he writes:

> The camera saves or isolates a set of appearances from the otherwise inevitable supercession of further appearances. It holds them unchanging. And before the camera, nothing else could do this, except, in the mind's eye, the faculty of memory (John Berger, p 18).

There is a question that nevertheless arises here: what sort of memory is it that the camera records? A photograph that depicts a 'happy' family which is in fact split by arguments, tension and authoritarianism is no different from, say, a photo by the American photographer Edward Weston of a vast factory rendered not as a workplace where people toil and profit is extracted, but as a complex geometry similar to a Gothic cathedral. A photo of a group of young males out for an evening sup-presses rivalry and sexuality in the same way an even older image, say, Rubens' city fathers get together for a group portrait, with their own rivalries laid aside for a time. In each case, the image produces a form of memory that takes an ideological form: the way 'one would like to be remembered'.

In this sense, looking at old photos — especially of oneself — can be a disconcerting experience, a form of recognition but also of misrecognition. On the one hand, the 'yes, that's me' follows from recog-nising oneself as a part of a particular history. But on the other hand, there is a sort of refusal to accept this history, so that a moment of identity with the image is immediately contradicted by a moment of the lack of such identity. Of this contradiction, Roland Barthes writes:

> Embracing the entire parental field, such imagery acts as a medium and puts me in relation to my body's *id*: it provokes in me a kind of obtuse dream, whose units are (rather than the family) teeth, hair, a nose, skinniness, long legs in knee-length socks that don't belong to me, though to no-one else: here, I am henceforth in a state of disturbing familiarity . . . It follows that the childhood photograph is both highly indiscreet (it is my body *from underneath* which is presented) and quite discreet (the photograph is not of 'me') (*Roland Barthes*, 1979).

As a kind of mirror the photograph reflects back a memory that is in disharmony with other forms of memory and experience; sufficient, if we are to believe the French psychoanalyst, Jacques Lacan, to cause a traumatic 'repetition' throughout the rest of one's life. Writing in 1948, Lacan proposed that children undergo a stage he called the 'mirror phase' (though the phase can be repeated in subsequent life) (J. Lacan, 1-7). In the mirror phase, the child, Lacan argues, begins to see itself ('as') in a mirror, that is, as a *representation* of itself. For Lacan, this is the first time the child sees itself as a whole body (an 'other') rather than as a collection of uncoordinated limbs and movements. But the moment of 'yes, that's me, there is me there in the mirror' gets immediately contradicted by the realisation that, no, that image in the mirror is not me. Lacan's conclusion — that our initial ideas of harmony and identification 'are constituted in disharmony' — is a scenario that Barthes repeats in his writing on childhood photos, and it leads Lacan on to a striking conclusion: that, as result of this initial mirror phase trauma in childhood, we keep repetitiously seeking out an ego-ideal that would perform this function. Taking it one step further, it is possible to say that processes of identification with movie, ad or fashion images perform just this function of arriving at an ideal identification with the image, thwarted in childhood and resought forever thereafter.

Lacan's theory is a powerful one (indeed, almost too 'pat' for its or our own good!). But it goes some way to getting to an understanding of how family snaps, not to mention advertising photography, work. In its rigorous agenda of sites on which such photos can take place (family 'celebrations', nights out, beach days), the amateur camera re-enacts overdetermined scenes, in a similar way to which one returns to the same places or sites/sights within dreams. This at least allows us to explain how amateur photographers learn other photographic techniques (whether from art or advertising photography), and go on to transform them for the uses described above: if 'overdetermination' is the condensation of a wide range of experiences and thoughts into single images, then amateur photography can be seen as taking up precisely this role — the reduction of wide spans of lived experience into a finite number of spaces for the visual representation of such experience.

As part of their actual technique, family photography, like any other image-making process, finally forces the subject of the photo to emit signs, as John Tagg has written. In family snaps, pose, glance, gaze and even the background props contribute to this — part of the subject's gesture that she or he submits to the image-making process. At the same time, it is worthwhile noting what people actually sometimes do when being snapped. When, for example, people (especially kids) pull faces, make unasked-for gestures or parody the 'appropriate' ones, they take the process of 'being imaged' to almost its logical extreme. The face-pulling moment not only tries to subvert the whole process of identification with the ritual of the family snap, but goes deeper. In effect, it registers a schizophrenic side to having one's picture taken — one in which one tries to escape from one's body and from the image — and history-making machines that surround and try to possess it.

Visual Metaphor

In the battle over credit cards that has been going on in Australia for the last few years, there has been a dramatic turnaround. Until recently, when credit card companies' willingness to supply a vast range of cards for all purposes bordered on promiscuity, the fashion was to have and be able to display a quantity of them. With Commonwealth Bank Mastercard, however, all this has changed: now the battle is for the *single* card to satisfy all needs. Mastercard, says Commonwealth, is 'all the cards (plural) you need'.

American Express's relationship has been The Gold Card. Its ad for The Gold Card features a seemingly perverse lack of detail or explanation (figure 5.3). It is as if the card were an art-object and the underlying words (The Gold Card) simply a title, as for a painting, sculpture or other exhibit. The implication is that gold, with all its connotations as the standard upon which currencies are based, transcends money and becomes value. Access to this connotation (gold = value, value that outlasts and transcends that of mere currency) is primarily through colour. (And here we can pause to think for a bit about the way in which colour reproduction, primarily in magazines but also in newspapers, has elevated colour symbolism to a major force not just in packaging, but also in

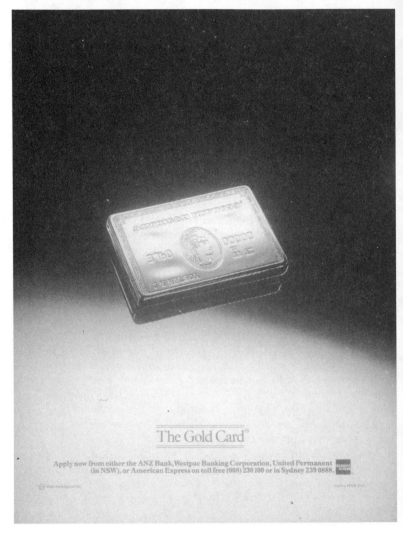

Visual metaphor: the transcendent value of gold

advertising images.) If, for example, you sometimes wonder about the prevalence of reds in successful products like Winfield, Marlborough or Coke, there is no lack of competing explanations.

A simple one was offered in the 1950s by E.H. Gombrich. 'In certain cultural contexts', wrote Gombrich, 'there are visual qualities that lend themselves to symbolic use' (Erich Gombrich, 1973). Thus, red, as the colour of flames or blood 'offers a metaphor for anything violent or strident'. For this theory, colour symbolism arises from a transference of a quality (redness) from one thing (blood/fire) to another (cigarettes or soft drinks). The process — properly called *metaphor* — endows the product with the tenor of the metaphor: violent or strident individuality (no mistake that Marlboro Country or Coke Is It campaigns always feature rigorously isolable, or even isolated, social groups like surfies or cowboys).

A slightly different approach might be not to look at colour symbolism as an isolated process working almost haphazardly within culture, but as a systematic process. Here, red is identified within a structure of colours arranged in oppositions. Optically, red, along with yellow and blue, is a primary colour. But systematically, it falls in the middle of a colour paradigm based on an antithesis of yellow/white and blue/black, in which red is a mediating colour, midway in a structure that is arranged yellow/ orange/red/violet/blue (J. Cirlot, 1962). This allows us to read off not only why red labels are the standard (Winfield Red, Johnny Walker Red Label), but also why milds are blue, that black labels are deluxe lines, or even that menthols (that combine yellow and blue, at the opposing ends of the sequence) are green. Clearly, in this theory, there is nothing intrinsic in the colour used that gives it meaning, but rather its place in the structure with regard to other colours, read as a series of oppositions.

Back to The Gold Card. Gombrich attributes the value connoted by gold to the fact that 'wealth can no longer be seen, that it no longer provides direct visual gratification' (as it did for say, richly-worked still life painting of former times). In the twelfth century, Gombrich notes, gold was associated with 'the light of God' that 'carries the mind from the material to the spiritual world'. Light as the manifestation of the divine in turn carried with it the notion that 'seeing cannot be separated from knowing' — and this ancient relay of ideas is what The Gold Card continues to draw on. Along with the long-running Benson and Hedges Gold series of photomontages, heavily reliant on selling cigarettes as prized art-objects, The Gold Card sets up gold as transcendent value. But again we should note that the process of signification does not simply draw on older connotations of gold; meaning is also carried by what gold is not. For B and H, the opposite is Sterling, a metal of lesser value and a smoke that comes in 25s; for The Gold Card, the substance to which it is the implied antithesis, is — dare we say — mere plastic, such as the other cards are made of.

Finally, a further development of American Express's campaign should be noted. As part of its cause-related marketing campaign, American Express is offering part of its profits to eradicating the *chlamydia psittaci* virus from the koala population. The disease, which makes koalas sterile and blind, will, American Express hopes, be fought by shaking dollars out of both American and Australian pockets by way of a donation by the company on every transaction involving American Express travellers' cheques.

In the 1930s de Reszke cigarettes in Australia used to sponsor an 'opera hour' on radio, with the intention of linking together a famous opera singer, good lungs and smoking. Similarly, as John Potts has noted, Wrigley's sponsored *Dad and Dave* in Australia to Australianise what was thought to be the 'dirty American habit' of chewing gum (John Potts, 1984). In competition with a number of Australian credit cards, American Express's choice of the koala is perhaps a choice along the same lines, achieving an indigenisation of an American service by helping koalas. At the same time, the koala development may not be as different a campaign as The Gold Card itself. Both appeal in their own way to a notion of scarcity — the scarcity of gold on the one hand, and impending scarcity of a national animal on the other. Different as the vehicle of the visual metaphor may be (gold, koala), the tenor (rarity/national treasure) is the same. Pity about the hairy-nosed wombat!

Visual Metonymy

One of the most widely circulated series of newsphotos in Australian history is that of the attempted departure from Australia in 1954 of Mrs Eudokia Petrov, the wife of Vladimir Petrov. Petrov himself had defected earlier that year to Australia, having previously held the position of Second Secretary to the Soviet Embassy in Canberra. Mrs Petrov, having, it seems, been in two minds about whether to go back to the USSR, stopped (or was stopped) in her journey at Darwin, and amongst the melee, lost her shoe. Held aloft by a member of the crowd, it took on a mythic status immediately — a Cinderella leaving her slipper at the ball, perhaps on the stroke of twelve. But, for a watching public, Mrs Petrov's shoe had another meaning. The shoe was made of alligator skin, and immediately was raised in status from something Mrs Petrov wore on her foot to the status of *sign*. For it signified that Mrs Petrov, unlike the other 'dowdy' women at the Soviet Embassy, was already 'western' — the alligator-skin shoe, with its connotations of 'style' and (sexual) display was suddenly an *indicator*. Something peripheral and incidental suddenly became the key to the understanding that Mrs Petrov (and, by implication, all Russians) would rather be western than communist. Whereas metaphor involves the condensation of one element into another (gold or koalas into value and treasure) metonymy involves the displacement of something, usually a detail, into the status of a whole — and usually a whole that could not be recognised as such. Thus, Mrs Petrov's shoe, an insignificant part of her attire, came to mean much more than she herself did in the political situation in which she was cast.

The technique of visual metonymy is well known from film: an image of marching feet indicates an army, perhaps; a hand opening a door signifies not only the body excluded from the image but also the intention of that body. The shoe, the feet, the hand are, in the image, displaced from the body, but seem to reveal more about what that body or person is about than actually showing the whole of that body. Visual metonymy can work by showing only a body part (eyes in a rear-vision mirror, as in the 'Under .05' ad, or hands, as in the 'Toast all Winter for Not Much Bread' ad for greater electricity use). But it can also work by including a detail that is usually suppressed, so that the detail becomes the main key for deciphering the image.

These two operations of metonymy can be contrasted in two (ingenious!) ads for Sheridan products. The first conforms to a more accepted use of metonymical technique. Captioned 'When Your Good Name Is On The Line', it features towels out to dry on a line. Above one of them can be glimpsed elbow-length gloves, and a forehead surmounted by a tiara. Since very few people wear tiaras in the general run of things (much less when hanging out the washing), we experience a gradual cancelling-out of options for meaning. The one most of us come up with — The Queen! — is contradicted by the domestic scene. What eventuates is a visual pun: the drawing together of two contradictory meanings that, nevertheless, must co-exist given the limited available interpretations. Hence the operation of the joke, and hence also the operation of metonymy — a relocation of meaning (and, in a way, a way of making meaning harder to get at), but also of making only one meaning available, unspeakable and obvious at the same time.

Another Sheridan ad, this time for sheets, has a young male stretched out under (yes) sheets which cover him up to his navel. His arms thrown back behind his head in repose, he appears, on one level, as a study of a sleeping male. Denotatively, all that it indicates is sleep. For the connotative level of the image, however, we have to direct away from the study to a point within the study that appears as gratuitous, incidental and unasked-for — but which conveys the main meaning of the image. Nearest the camera and most prominent in colour-contrast terms is an armpit — but an armpit in which the hairs are matted and soaked with sweat. A wide narrative thus is implied where none was before (aftermath of work, sex, or both) — and all on the 'chance' perception of this unavoidable detail. By the quality of something essentially metonymical — the observation of the existence, quality and consistency of the armpit — the image gets elevated into the status of film 'still', with narrative included on both sides. As with Mrs Petrov's shoe, something 'private' and usually unobservable has become the central point of access into the scene which the narrative implies (but, coyly and disingenuously refuses). Access via the metonym thus is available only through complicity and a form of reading that bears directly on the work put in by the viewer.

Another way of putting this might be to say that the image operates on a code that allows the viewer to skip from recognising 'what is there' to recognising the *meaning* of 'what is there'. In the earliest writing of the French theorist Roland Barthes on the subject of the photographic message, he described the photo as 'a message without a code' (*Image-Music-Text*) — and this is on one level true enough. The photo seems to be just an analogue (a rendering of masses, volumes and spaces that were its subject), but within this there are runaway details that subversively spell out a far greater significance for the image than those inherent in the mere and humble business of snapping something. Later in his career, in the 1980 book *Camera Lucida*, Barthes backed away slightly from the 'message without a code' idea by proposing that within some photographic images (if not all — as with most news-photos), there could be a distinction between a *studium* — the 'obvious' construction of meaning — and a *punctum*, the jokes 'aside' the photo makes.

Trivial as it at first might seem, the *punctum*, ('point', detail) is what the image may be all about:

> The *punctum* shows no preference for morality or good taste: The *punctum* can be ill-bred . . . What I notice, by that additional vision which is in a sense the gift, the grace of the *punctum*, is (for instance) a hand resting on a door-frame: a large hand whose nails are anything but clean (*Camera Lucida*, 41).

For Barthes, the *punctum* 'while, paradoxically, remaining a "detail", fills the whole picture'. Writing of the Robert Mapplethorpe photo *Young Man With Arm Extended*, Barthes writes: 'The photographer has caught the boy's hand . . . at just the right degree of openness, the right density of abandonment . . . The *punctum* is, then, a kind of subtle *boy and . . .*' In Mapplethorpe's photo it is the armpit (private to the subject, the key to the observer's looking at something which is private but which becomes public via the necessity of the photo to realise its primary mandate to be intimate) that gives it its bloom. (Armpits are reputed to smell; as do shoes!)

Metonymy is above all disclosure: a privileged view that, although available to everyone who sees it, manages to personalise the view for all involved — as much for the photographic subject as for the viewer. When Mick Jagger's armpit appeared on the cover of *Rolling Stone* (and Prince's later, in 1984) it constituted a 'scandalous' revelation. At the same time, the 'inadvertence' of the revelation was not only *a* meaning, but (as with the joke) the *only* meaning. Since then, taking in along the way the exposure of Patti Smith's armpit on the cover of *Easter*, an especially tabooed glimpse since women are supposed to shave there, we have a series of metonymical displacements/replacements. The latest is Madonna's navel — a *punctum* if ever there was one!

To bring the discussion back to a momentarily serious level, it can be noted that the glorification of the underside, negative or hidden aspect of a product involves an inversion of values that has long been part of the codes of advertisers themselves. One of these tenets, attributed to David Ogilvy of the major advertising agency Ogilvy and Mather, holds that if a product has a negative element to it, then the advertiser should isolate this element (rather than suppress it), and then turn it into the major product selling point. Thus, in an age of anti-smoking graffiti such as 'Smoker's Stink', Alpine sells on a 'Fresh is Alpine' slogan. Cottee's orange cordial advertises using scenes of orchards, saying 'Now Cottee's is putting more oranges in their cordial, we have to grow more oranges'. Under fire from a consumer market worried about refined additives, the sugar industry advertises sugar as 'a natural part of life'. Similarly, Lufthansa, conscious that all 747s are basically the same in design and use, advertises itself by an 'authentic passenger statement' on Lufthansa's paint-jobs: 'The outside of a plane tells you a lot about the inside'. Widely diverse as all these examples are, they all basically work on metonymical displacement. Working from an attribute or detail (whether trivial or downright negative), a leap is made to a whole, in which the beside-the-point becomes, triumphantly, *the* point.

Further Reading

Barthes, R *Elements of Semiology* Hill and Wang 1967
——— 'The Photographic Message' in Stephen Heath ed *Image-Music-Text* Fontana 1977
——— *Roland Barthes* Hill and Wang 1979

Barthes, R 1977 *The Eiffel Tower* Hill and Wang 1979
———— *Camera Lucida* Hill and Wang 1982
Benjamin, W 'The Author as Producer, in Benjamin *Understanding Brecht* New Left Books 1977
Berger, J *Ways of Seeing* Penguin 1978
Cirlot, J E *A Dictionary of Symbols* RKP 1962/83
Debord, G *The Society of Spectacle* Detroit 1983
Gombrich, E H 'Illusion and Visual Deadlock' in *Meditations on a Hobby Horse* Phaidon 1973
Kristeva, J *Desire in Language* Blackwells 1980
Lacan, J 'The Mirror Phase' in Lacan *Ecrits* Tavistock 1977
Potts, J *The Price You Pay: Advertising and Commercial Radio in Australia* MA thesis NSWIT 1984

CHAPTER SIX

V

The Moving Image: Film and Television

by
Anne Cranny-Francis

The last two chapters have dealt with the construction of texts in a single medium: language in the case of Chapter Four, and visual images in Chapter Five. This, the final chapter, discusses texts composed of a number of media: language, visual images, music and other sound, colour and light. Beyond that complexity, and above all, these texts unfold in time; a time of various duration and not in the viewer/reader/listener's control. Given that everything culturally produced has meaning, it will be clear that texts of this kind display a density and complexity of meaning beyond that of texts in one medium.

The vast complexities of social structures and of their contradictions are everywhere evident in these texts, no matter how innocent their appearance. All texts are interweaves of ideological strands of diverse — though not unpredictable — kind. This chapter attempts to demonstrate the complexities of the meanings of these texts, but above all provides a means of understanding the processes that lead to the production of these texts, and the equally complex processes of their reception, reading and reconstruction by the reader. Both the mechanisms that work to conceal the fragmentary nature of texts, and those that permit that fragmentation to appear are encompassed in Anne Cranny-Francis' term 'faultless fragmentation'. From one point of view — that of the ideologue — a faultless text is one that appears unproblematic, of one piece, obvious, natural. From another point of view — that of the critical producer or the critical reader — texts that draw attention to their fragmentary constitution are faultless, for they give insights to reader/viewers which take them beyond common sense to a more adequate understanding of the functioning of texts, and of the society that has produced them.

Last and by no means least, this chapter addresses a point that has been largely left implicit in this book so far. That is the matter of pleasure. Many texts are produced for the reader or viewer's pleasure. They are not meant to be particularly serious as entertainment; they are meant to be fun, to give joy, bring diversion, take the viewer or reader into a world beyond that of the everyday. But the fact that such texts are not meant (by whom, one should ask) to be serious, may make their effects more telling, their meanings more easy to take in, more difficult to resist. It may be that ideology is most effective when nothing at all seems to be at issue.

And so this chapter looks at texts which are not 'serious', which are 'just' entertainment: science fiction, adventure films, soap operas. Anne Cranny-Francis shows these texts as highly complex, highly mannered; and she shows their audiences to be highly sophisticated, aware of conventions and willing to enjoy and manipulate them. No duped housewives here, unable to respond to these fictions other than to treat them as realistic accounts of the world. In this and in other ways this chapter opens up a rich and subtle network of paths to an understanding of the commodities produced by the cultural industries, and through that, to an understanding of society and culture.

Visual Text and its Conventions

The society in which we live is saturated with visual representations, with images of the real — in photographs, billboard advertisements, television and film. The media of film and television must be counted the major sources of both entertainment and information about our society available to most people. Not that the information function of the visual media is often acknowledged. That is usually assigned specifically to documentary and news programs. Yet in representing ourselves to ourselves, as film and television do, these media are constantly (re) introducing and reinforcing the assumptions, beliefs, values and ideologies, by and from which our society is constructed. This 'ideological information' comes to us not only through documentaries and the news, but also in adventures, telemovies and soap operas. In film it has a fundamental structuring function, in serious social realist movies such as *Newsfront* and *Strikebound*, as well as in popular films such as the *Mad Max* trilogy. And that information is active not only in narrative incidents, but in the conventions by which the narrative is constructed. Futhermore, these ideologies inform the genres into which these narratives are subsequently subsumed: genres such as soap opera, Western, science fiction, current affairs and so on.

When we attempt to understand texts, when we act as critics of film and television texts, we have to consider all these aspects of the production of 'moving pictures': narrative structures, generic conventions, ideological functions and assumptions embodied in the text. In a sense we are extending the analysis of 'image' presented in the previous chapter to include analysis of the organisation of the image into an extended narrative (or non-narrative) structure, with a particular generic category (or categories) to produce a complex audiovisual text. As previous chapters have insisted (particularly Chapters Two and Three), we have to consider the nature of the society in which the text was produced, its economic imperatives, the ideological discourses that describe and define it. We have to analyse the production practices (e.g. editing, lighting, camera shots) that determined its formation. And we have to consider the audience for which it was designed. The notion that a film or television program can have a transparent or obvious meaning is, therefore, hopelessly inadequate. Meaning arises in the complex interaction between text or representation, audience, and the society in which it is viewed.

In this chapter I shall attempt to deal with the complex issues that arise when one attempts to analyse a film or television program. Along the way I shall refer to several specific film and television texts, which are widely accessible, to illustrate my argument. And I shall also consider particular kinds of programs such as soap opera, a form of television genre which is currently the focus of much debate about television and popular film, about their interest for and influence on their audience.

Society represented in Metropolis *(1925), forerunner to* Thunderdome, *by Kennedy/Miller*

Film and Television

Before I start talking about the analysis of film and television programs, it is worth considering whether the same critical categories can be used with the two media. I believe they can, though with some provisos. It seems to me that there are several critical concepts, which I shall go on to discuss in this chapter, that are useful and appropriate with many kinds of texts: verbal, visual and audiovisual (e.g. books, painting, sculpture, advertising, film, television). But in each case it is crucial that the material determinants of the particular form of representation under analysis be considered and incorporated into the discussion, if a comprehensive critique is to be achieved. So, with film and television, we as critics have to be aware that very different economic imperatives operate in the two media, which profoundly affect the finished product.

Not that this awareness should lessen or soften the critique. However, it can place into context choices made in the production of a particular (film or television) text. And it helps the critic to understand the compromises that operate in the production of a text, whether it be film or television, or a book or painting or advertisement. In negotiating these compromises the critic becomes aware of the extraordinarily complex nature of the text. With film and television the critic is alerted to the compromises engendered by the visual nature of the media. And it is crucial to understand that film and television programs are not reducible to written scripts, that the significances or meanings of these forms of representation are generated as much, or more, by the visuals. So in using particular critical categories we have to apply them not only to the words spoken by the actors, or even to the sequence of events that constitutes the story, but also to the *way* the story is told. The significance or meaning of a female character, for example, rests not only with what she says or does, but with how she is dressed, how she is positioned by the camera, which actress is chosen for the role, and so on. It seems as if I am setting the critic a task of almost overwhelming complexity, and I suppose I am. But it is important to begin the discussion with an understanding of the complexities of the texts with which we are dealing.

Discourse

I begin now with one of the concepts used in the analysis of texts, and that is discourse. Even though that term was introduced earlier, in Chapter Four in the section called 'Institutions and Ways of Talking', it may be helpful to give another brief account here. Both film and television programs are representations of the 'real', whether as naturalistic recreations of the real or as texts that focus on ideas or issues or emotions fundamental to the real. As such these texts inevitably reproduce those discourses that define for us what we have come to see as our real.

> Discourses are systematically organised sets of statements that give expression to the meanings and values of an institution. Beyond that, they define, describe and delimit what it is possible to say and not possible to say (and by extension — what it is possible to do or not to do) with respect to the area of concern of that institution, whether marginally or centrally. A discourse provides a set of possible statements about a given area, and organises and gives structure to the manner in which a particular topic, object, process is to be talked about. In that it provides descriptions, rules, permissions and prohibitions of social and individual actions. (G. Kress, 1985)

So discourses are sets of statements — verbal, visual or otherwise —

Workers of Metropolis, *underground, powerless slaves to technology and its controllers: discourse defining workers' role*

that give expression to the meanings and values of an institution, to the power relations that operate within and define that institution. This might be an institution of knowledge, such as modern science, or a way of dealing with social relationships, such as sexism. Each text, like society itself, is an interweave, a dialogue, of such discourses. Sometimes they reinforce or harmonise with each other; at other times they coexist in conflict or disharmony. The one text can be host to different and conflicting discourses. For example, it is not unusual now to find feminist and anti-feminist (or sexist) discourses together in the one text.

In *Star Wars*, the first film of the Lucas trilogy, both feminist and anti-feminist discourses coexist. At first appearance Princess Leia, the character around whom these discourses revolve, was something of a shock to viewers. She was not blonde, demure and simpering; she was strong, witty, and though not unattractive, definitely not a stereotypical beauty. In many ways she challenged viewers' assumptions about women and femininity, though of course her appeal was based on viewers' implicit acceptance of traditional female roles. Nevertheless, Princess Leia did point to a reassessment of those traditional roles. She was an active participant in all the adventures and she had a calmness and rationality her male companions lacked. *But*, Leia was also the princess of fairytale, as her title indicates, waiting to be rescued by her handsome prince and his offsider/helper. She was dressed all in white, in a fairytale gown, and had elaborately coiffured hair, in true aristocratic style.

We can deconstruct the image of Leia in a manner similar to the decoding of advertisements in the previous chapter, though there are more factors to be taken into account with the image or the character of a filmed text. As I said earlier, costume and make-up are highly significant. They place the character within the range of images appropriate to women, according to a particular ideology. Leia's costume and make-up are appropriate to a demure, romantic image of womanhood in a patriarchal order. Which is not to say that the character is necessarily constrained or confined by this image, but it is fundamental to the characterisation. The choice of actor is also crucial to a particular role because the actor brings with her/him the reverberations of other well-known roles to a particular part. In the case of Leia, Carrie Fisher was not a widely-known actress outside Hollywood, not a 'star', and so the part of Leia was largely a production of this film alone (compare with this the weight of previous roles, the reverberations, brought to the movie by Alec Guinness and Peter Cushing!). Other factors we might consider include the character's name (especially in a movie populated by Skywalkers and Solos), the character's musical theme, or the framing of the character by the camera.

Rather than proceed with an in-depth study of Leia of *Star Wars* however, I want to look instead briefly at a recent Australian film that also (re)presents conflicting images of women, the Kennedy-Miller production, *Mad Max Beyond Thunderdome (Mad Max 3)*. In *Mad Max 3* there are two main female characters, Bartertown's Aunty Entity and Savannah Nix, one of the feral children. The names of the characters are allegorical: Aunty Entity controls the law in Bartertown, that is, the kind of being or entity of its citizens (though not that being itself, so her relationship is not that of Mother — or Master); Savannah Nix lives in the wasteland, a tragic negation of savannah which has all been destroyed by nuclear war (the 'Pox-Eclipse' in the children's language). Aunty Entity is played by Tina Turner, a well-known singer whose stage act has characterised her as a strong, sexually attractive woman. Her costuming and make-up for *Mad Max 3* reinforce this image. As Aunty she wears a chainmail costume with deep decolletage, cut-away skirt (like her stage costumes) and 'feminine' accessories including bracelets, earrings and headband in matching silver. The costume is designed to be

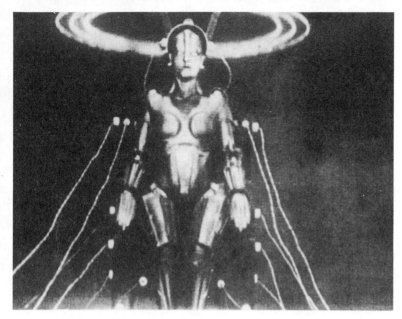

The Metropolis *robot: dangerous sexual potency under restraint*

sexy, revealing and feminine — supposedly constructed from material left over from the war. Her costume is a constant reminder that she survived and prospered after catastrophe. The fact that she is black is integral to the character, blacks in America having to be crisis survivors to prosper in that society. But this film was set in Australia, so why should an American black actress have this part?

No doubt there are economic reasons for this piece of casting (such as the need to appeal to the huge American audience, an attempt to win Turner's 'pop star' following, and, in the first place, the need to woo the movie's potential financial backers with strong casting), but how does the character function in an Australian setting? What does this choice of actress signify about Australian society — multiculturalism, colonialism, or colonisation? The character has platinum blonde, elegantly styled hair, an apparent contradiction: a black woman with the hair of a white beauty queen. Or does this mass of contradictions, this overdetermination of the sexy, strong woman stereotype — the wicked queen of *Snow White*, Mildred Pierce, Alexis of *Dynasty* — suggest a deliberate play with the conventions of this kind of characterisation, a deconstruction of this (patriarchal) image of women?

Savannah Nix looks very different from Aunty. Where Aunty is dressed, in the context of the post-holocaust society, as the sophisticate, Savannah is the natural woman, unsophisticated but charming. She is anorexically, fashionably slim and delicate, with elfin features (another meaning of Nix), and her 'naturalness' is both produced and signified by her costume of skins and leather (recycled goods like Aunty's chainmail). Like all the children her hair is dressed with clayey mud and her make-up is completed in tones that produce a suntanned appearance. Savannah's costume is cut high on the thigh, though this seems to have utilitarian purpose in the 'Crack in the Earth' where she lives as a hunter (at least there is this 'logical' possibility, as against the flamboyant sexuality and physical impracticality — chainmail under a desert sun could not be very comfortable — of Aunty's costume). We do not see as many lingering close-ups of Savannah, as we do of Aunty, shots which draw attention to and objectify her body. Savannah seems to be characterised as much by loving and caring as by sexuality, as in her greeting of her son, Finn McCoo when she returns with Max, and the 'madonna and child' shot of her at the end of the movie. So is Savannah the natural, 'good' woman, where Aunty is the 'civilised', corrupt, 'bad' woman? This conclusion is suggested by the initial appearance of the characters, and by their music themes: Aunty's entry heralded by languorous saxophone music, Savannah's by an exotic mixture of wind and percussion instruments. Yet these signifiers cannot be considered out of context. Just as the characterisation of Princess Leia involved consideration of her role in the narrative, as both active participant and helpless victim (princess of the fairytale 'quest' narrative), so the narrative roles of Aunty and Savannah are also fundamental to their characterisations; and those characterisations are crucial to the analysis of feminist and/or anti-feminist discourse in the film.

Narrative

I now wish to introduce another concept important for us as critics, and that is narrative. The narrative of a text inevitably involves a transformation, a change. Within the text the viewer witnesses a movement through conflict (between characters, character and incident) to a resolution. In making this movement, this transformation process — accessible and coherent to viewers — conservative ideological discourses are incorporated into the text. That is, discourses with which the viewer is familiar and (usually) comfortable are incorporated into the narrative so that the transformation seems obvious, simple and transparent. Stephen Heath summarises this double function of the narrative in this way: narrative, he says, 'is not only the story; it is also the process by which that story is made intelligible to viewers.'

Consider, for example, the 'quest' narrative, the fairytale narrative, which is the basis of so many films and television programs. In his study of fairytale Vladimir Propp structurally analysed the quest narrative, designating the components that occur with the regularity of convention. These components include: a 'good' person (the hero) in conflict with an 'evil' person (the villain) over a passive victim(s), which Propp identified as 'the princess and her father'. And there are various other subsidiary roles: helper, donor, false hero, and so on. *Star Wars* is structured by this quest narrative: Luke Skywalker is the hero and the victim/princess are Princess Leia and her father, the ruler of Aldebaran (destroyed by the Death Star); the villain is Darth Vader (or a combination of Vader and the Peter Cushing character, the Grand Moff Tarkin). Traditionally these narratives have been read as a dual quest: the hero's quest to save the princess being an essential part of his quest to find himself, his own identity. And the Lucas trilogy goes on to develop the 'inner quest' motif in the second and third films (*The Empire Strikes Back* and *Return of the Jedi*), where Luke learns that Darth Vader is his father and so has to confront his own potential for evil and for corruption.

Ideological discourses colonise these narratives at various points, particularly those involving the distribution of power. This is not surprising since recognition of power structures, and the power discourses that identify them, are fundamental to our understanding our own society and our ability to live in this society. These discourses are part of the process by which the story is made intelligible to viewers. In *Star Wars* one of the discourses readily accessible to viewers is a sexist discourse about women and femininity, which defines women as weak, helpless, powerless, emotional and unreliable. And interestingly, that discourse is not only a construction of image (wardrobe, make-up, lighting, etc), it is also a structural function of the narrative story. The story places Leia in a helpless, subordinate, powerless role. As I noted earlier, Vladimir Propp actually specified the victim role by gender: 'a princess (a sought-for person) and her father'. Theoretically, the possibility that the victim is male exists, yet it must be highly significant that Propp's primary specification identifies this role as female. *Star Wars* in its very structure incorporates a discourse about the power available and appropriate to women and men; that is, available and appropriate according to a conservative, patriarchal discourse describing female and male behaviour. This film incorporates, structurally, a sexist discourse that places men in the position of hero (active, rational, powerful) and women in that of victim. In fact the humour in *Star Wars* often comes from the conflict, the disjunction between Leia's assertive behaviour and her (passive) structural function. The consequences of this structural tagging of female and male roles are far-reaching. We, as viewers, are familiar and (usually) comfortable with the established (patriarchal) social order, so that conventions grounded in its discourses are unproblematic for us. We do not even notice that they are conventions; they have come to seem natural to us. Fiction that attempts to undermine these conventions and the discourses they incorporate tends, therefore, to be perceived as disruptive, alien, uncomfortable.

Film-makers, television producers, writers and artists, whose aim it is to challenge established, conservative discourses such as patriarchy, often find their works compromised by the conventions they use (and which often identify those texts for audiences). The discourses carried by the conventions may undermine the social criticism expressed elsewhere in the story. Conversely, the text producer might attempt to undermine the convention, but risks the discomfort, the alienation of her/his audience. *Mad Max 3* is also structured by the quest narrative. Max's quest for identity, his 'inner quest', is a crucial plot line, while the story also involves him in a series of conflicts which situate him as the hero. In one of these conflicts Aunty Entity is the villain. The character of Aunty as evil is constructed in the film via a whole chain of significations organised around the representation of the Law. Aunty *is* the Law in Bartertown but, as her aerial apartments signify, it is a Law that is *above* the people, not *of* the people. As the Law, Aunty hires Max as a mercenary to kill her opposition, the muscle (Blaster) who protects the technological genius (Master). This act is contextualised through Max by reference to (the audience's) conventional standards of morality. It is Max who sardonically describes Aunty's behaviour as 'real civilised', with the all-too-apparent implication that it is not; that this behaviour is uncivilised, barbaric, anarchic — qualities conventionally associated with evil. Later, when Max refuses to kill Blaster, Aunty's manipulation of the crowd's chant (from 'Two men enter. One man leaves' to 'Bust a deal, face the wheel') is a revelation not only about the fickleness of the public, in many senses their (our) corruptibility, but also of the corruption of Aunty herself. This set of significations is completed by the killing of the helpless Blaster, now revealed as intellectually retarded, childlike. Aunty's role as villain is confirmed by these incidents and her role in them. The conflict that structures this part of the film is that between Aunty and Max; it is this conflict that produces a resolution (Max's banishment). So how does this characterisation of Aunty relate to the discourses of power and gender already discussed? Is a powerful female villain permissible within the discourses of patriarchy?

The answer to the latter question is a resounding Yes! Ever since Lilith was unceremoniously ejected from the Garden of Eden, the 'evil woman' has been a female stereotype. She is the active, assertive woman, the one who will not accept her (under patriarchy, ideologically approved) position of subservience, humility and passivity. Rosemary Jackson, in her book on Fantasy, writes:

> The shadow on the edges of bourgeois culture is variously identified, as black, mad, primitive, criminal, socially deprived, deviant, crippled, or (when sexually assertive) female. Difficult or unpalatable social realities are distorted through many literary fantasies to emerge as melodramatic shapes: monsters, snakes, bats, vampires, dwarfs, hybrid beasts, devils, reflections, *femmes fatales*. (R. Jackson, 1982)

Aunty is a version of that *femme fatale* and, as such, she is constitutionally evil. Her characterisation as villain, her narrative role, is both ideologically determined and ideologically approved. Female characters can occupy roles that are positions of power, but the characters are almost invariably evil and they are almost invariably defeated. Ideology and narrative comply in producing the powerful role appropriate to a female character.

Analysis of the narrative roles of Leia and Aunty shows not only the complexity of the films under discussion, but also the interaction between ideology and narrative. In each case the narrative roles can be seen to respond in part to (patriarchal) ideological representations of women, of the victim and of the female villain. Most importantly it can be seen that these roles are not gender-free. To operate effectively within the signifying system of a particular society they must be intelligible to the members of that society, and one way of making them intelligible is to structure them according to the ideological assumptions and practices of that society.

Of course, that does not limit the narrative roles completely; many texts, like *Star Wars* and *Mad Max 3*, incorporate non-traditional, non-conservative elements in their texts, in their delineations of roles, perhaps as a response to progressive discourses operating within a conservative ideological domain. The motive for this responsiveness need not be political activism; it might be an intelligent respect for the

Femmes-fatale: assertive and dangerous

audience. So it might be asked, at this point, whether other features of the text are likely to influence or be influenced by audience response to a text, a film or television program.

Genre

As you will have noted by now, texts are highly conventionalised productions. Producers rely on audience familiarity with these conventions, incorporating that recognition into their construction of a text. Sometimes they reproduce a familiar convention exactly, so that the audience is comfortable with the text; at other times, they deliberately contradict it, to produce responses ranging from fear to laughter. I have already talked about conventions of narrative. Another range of conventions includes the structure of the text, the kinds of characters and incidents used, even patterns of dialogue. These conventions organise texts into particular classes or *genres*. My discussion of this term follows on from that put forward in Chapter Four. Here I am particularly concerned to show the importance of this concept in relation to film and video.

Most people are familiar with the names of the genres of film and television, such as western, science fiction (SF), soap opera, thriller, romance, documentary. Each of these genres has specific characteristics that identify it. The problem with writing about genre is that virtually no text shows the characteristics of only one genre, although one genre often predominates. So what is the point of the category, genre; what use is it to the critic?

The generic composition of a text can tell the critic much about both its construction and the audience response to it. The film-maker's choice of particular genre(s), based on her/his perception of audience response, may enable the critic to guess the intention of the film-maker, though this is obviously difficult ground. A film-maker may have a different notion from the critic of the audience response elicited by particular generic conventions. Guessing intentions is fraught with danger! The critic can, however, evaluate the dialogic interactions and political consequences of generic conventions in a text. S/he can trace the social and political realities these conventions mediate and discuss their representation within particular genres.

Star Wars and *Mad Max 3* both exhibit the generic conventions of science fiction. Both are structured by the quest narrative, which is commonly associated with science fiction. In a genre primarily about discovery — of the new, the other, the alien, the self — the quest narrative is clearly appropriate. Its major character is led through conflict — with aliens, the other, her/himself — to a resolution that involves a metamorphosis; reconciliation with the alien, the other, the self; self-knowledge. At least this is the theoretical description of SF. But we have already seen how the quest narrative is colonised by ideological discourses, so that it is highly contentious whether SF ever achieves this elevated aim of self-knowledge. Both the theorists and the apologists of or for SF consistently ignore its political assumptions and implications. *Star Wars* might be about Luke Skywalker's self-discovery, his recognition of the potential for evil within himself, represented by his father, Darth Vader. And it might also be a crude representation of the oedipal conflict between father and son, which is theorised as structuring the boy's entry into society. But it is also structured and colonised throughout by the kind of individualist ideology that has been seen more recently in films like *Rambo*. And as a cinematic representation of the propaganda of the recent political regime in the U.S.A. it is unsurpassed. Much to the disgust (ironically?) of its producer/director, George Lucas, President Reagan has appropriated the name of the movie as part of the political justification for his own satellite defence [sic] program. Which shows as much about the communication skills of the former actor as it does about *Star Wars*, the movie. The point I am making here is a very simple one, that a SF film, set in a galaxy far far away, is a product of this society and so is as revealing about this society as any other kind of film. The quest narrative conventional in SF texts is, as I have already discussed, a site in which ideological assumptions and practices can be detected.

Science fiction films have other identifying characteristics, of course. One of the most common conventions is the alien: the Jawas, mammoths, Chewbacca, the bar creatures of *Star Wars*; Mr Spock of television's *Star Trek*, *Doctor Who*'s Daleks. These creatures signify to an audience that the genre is SF. *Star Wars* adds interstellar travel, spaceships, intelligent robots, strange worlds, a death star, and sundry other technological marvels to reinforce its other-worldly futuristic setting. This over-determination of the futuristic, the overtly fictional, should alert critics to the consequences (social, political) of this apparent removal of the narrative from the category of the 'real'.

I have already discussed the contradictory representations of femininity represented in *Star Wars*. Suffice it to say that *Star Wars* was written and produced during a very active period of feminist writing, when the other-worldly, alien conventions of the SF genre were being used to construct a subversive critique of male-dominated patriarchal ideologies. Lucas' very gentle incorporation of the same critique in *Star Wars* needs to be evaluated in relation to discourses incorporated via other SF conventions. The technological wizardry of *Star Wars*, both on and off the screen, participates inevitably in the discourses about science and technology that dominate our society. And those discourses are often overtly misogynistic. They proceed from claims of objectivity, the concept used to mystify the economic and social consequences of scientific and technological change. This 'objectivity' is evaluated positively in relation to 'subjectivity', which is then related simplistically to human functioning via equations of logic/emotion, male/female. Women are equated with emotion, lack of logic, subjectivity. They cannot handle (for which read: are excluded from) the technological and scientific structures and functions of our society, which become an aggressively male preserve. It seems likely, therefore, that Lucas' mild critique of sexism will be subsumed by the more strident repudiation of women coded into discourses about technology.

Multi-Generic Texts

At the beginning of this discussion I made the point that texts rarely exhibit the conventions of just one genre. Rather, several different genres will be articulated within the one text, each carrying particular significance(s) for the audience and interacting with other genres represented. *Mad Max 3* begins with a pyrotechnic display of generic mixing, the apparent aim of which is the characterisation of the text's eponymous hero, Max. Max first appears heavily concealed in nomadic desert robes, driving a camel train; he is the wanderer, the Sheik, a romantic figure, alone, and powerful in his aloneness, his self-sufficiency. Then, in a scene reminiscent of Hitchcock's *North by North-West* he is buzzed by a light aircraft; he is the victim of an unwarranted attack, eliciting audience sympathy (like his predecessor, Cary Grant). His camel train is stolen by the pilot of the aircraft and, as he runs after it, his face mask falls back to reveal the attractive features of Max Rockatansky, driver, road warrior, loner, a man obsessed by the loss of all he loved, his family. In *Mad Max 1* and *Mad Max 2* he was the chief player of a modern revenge tragedy, like all those Clint Eastwood characters, out to revenge the loss of their loved ones. But in *Mad Max 2* Max had his revenge, so is that role still relevant? And he is also 'Mel Gibson', film star, who brings to this role inflections or touches of the other roles he has played, as lover, adventurer, idealist, coward, soldier. Next, the character is seen from the thighs down, walking, in a shot from many westerns, perhaps most memorably *Shane*, the story of a cowboy who learns to love others, who undergoes a spiritual quest. True to that inflection, Max reaches down to retrieve his lost boots, leather cowboy boots. He removes a

Prince: character constructed through generic layering and confrontation

curved silver whistle, in place of the customary knife, from the side of his boot and, as he brings the whistle to his lips, we see that his hair is long and matted: he is the very personification of a 'Jesus in black leather', as Gibson once characterised the role. With his long hair, dishevelled appearance and dusty robes he is the saviour in the wasteland, the mad hermit, the wanderer, the prophet (for instance, Obi Wan Kenobi in *Star Wars*). Then in a brilliant rejection of realism Max is shown blowing the whistle as night falls; the sky darkens from daylight to dark on that one note, while Max stands silhouetted against the sky. The result is a 'genreflection' to all those images of a man alone against the sky, from Christ on the Cross and Moses on Mount Sinai to less exalted social radicals; he is the Romantic hero, the man at odds with society, whose rules he no longer accepts. The fantastic status of the text is established in that scene. So this Max is a compendium of Valentino, Cary Grant, Shane, Clint Eastwood, John the Baptist, Max Rockatansky, Christ, and probably many others. The character is not constructed by literal description or statement, but by inflection of generic conventions, genres of romance, Western, revenge tragedy, biblical epic, road movie, fantasy.

The same kind of generic complexity can be detected in most texts, though in *Mad Max 3* it has a structuring function. At the beginning of Spielberg's *Indiana Jones and the Temple of Doom* the main characters are involved in a fight at a nightclub called the Club Obi Wan, a homage by Spielberg to Lucas' *Star Wars* trilogy. In a film about a character whose first film was a film about films (i.e. *Raiders of the Lost Ark*) this kind of simple cross-referencing prepares the viewer for a very mannered film, concerned primarily with the techniques of film-making. The reference helps establish the genre of the film, rather than directing the viewer to particular generic conventions.

Intertextuality

In other films the cross-referencing has an intertextual function; that is, the producer utilises the associations of a particular generic structure or character or incident to augment or expand the significance of her/his own text. Consider, for example, the helicopter scene at the conclusion of John Carpenter's homage to Spielberg film, *Starman*. Echoing *Close Encounters of the Third Kind* and *E.T.: The Extra-Terrestrial*, Carpenter has his friendly alien pursued by the military with orders to capture and dissect (he even incorporates the grisly mortuary table from E.T.). As the Starman flees, Carpenter's helicopters rise menacingly over a ridge and then fly in pack formation, less like the noisy and rather blundering helicopters of *Close Encounters* than like those of *Apocalypse Now* with their ambiguous significances of Wagnerian delight in power alongside condemnations of its misuse. This ambiguity has then to be placed in the context of the entire film. What are we being shown about SF films and about Spielberg's films in particular? Is Carpenter championing Spielberg's apparently anti-authoritarian stance in films such as *The Sugarland Express, Close Encounters* and *E.T.*, or questioning his response to high technology? The placement of this generic scene — conventionally found in war movies, particularly 'macho' films glorifying war — in a SF film should alert the critic to possible correspondences between the genres; should prompt a fundamental examination of the ideological assumptions of both. So generic intertextuality can have a subversive or radical function within a text, because it can alert the critical viewer to similarities between genres which apparently have very different interests and aims.

This intertextuality may also serve to conceal the ideological assumptions of a text, welding together contradictory elements into an apparently seamless whole. How many viewers will take the trouble to tease out the characterisation of Max Rockatansky, to examine the ideological assumptions and significances of its component elements? What is it that holds this multigeneric text together? In the case of *Mad Max 3* and many other texts the invisible stitching is performed by the ubiquitous quest narrative. Writing about television narrative Len Masterman notes:

> Finally, mention must be made of one of television's dominant techniques for shaping the events it handles: the use of narrative. Television tells stories. News, current affairs programs, documentaries, sports programs, all create little dramas with their own heroes, villains, conflicts, reversals, rewards and resolutions — and they can easily be analysed in these terms. Dramatic shaping is endemic to most forms of editing for television, and it's probably most sensible to regard even the most factual documentaries, for example, as primarily *fictional* in form. But the dominant fiction which underpins the media's penchant for narrative is that there does indeed exist an unproblematic and disinterested 'position' from which the story may be told. In the deathless words of a former President of C.B.S. News, 'Our reporters do not cover stories from their point of view. They are presenting them from nobody's point of view'.

Hence the strength of Christopher Williams' assertion that 'narrative militates against knowledge ... because it attempts to conceal itself, to imply that this is how the world is'. But as we have seen, 'how the world is' *contains* the positions fed to the viewer by editing, framing, commentary, visual codings, etc. This militates against knowledge not because of 'bias' or the suppression or demotion of alternative viewpoints, but because what is concealed is the notion of the text as a site for the construction of meanings which should be considered and analysed in relation to the position, interests and intentions of their producers.

I have quoted Masterman at some length because it seems to me his description of the function of the narrative applies to all narrative texts, not just to television. The narrative structure itself conceals the material determinants of the text, including the generic conventions by which it is structured. This concealment works actively against viewer recognition of the fragmentary nature of the text, apprehension of which may well produce a viewer position critical of the transformation fundamental to the text. In considering the function of generic conversions in a text, therefore, it is necessary to consider also their incorporation/utilisation/use of a narrative which mediates the impact on the viewer of particular conventions and the ideological discourses they sustain. It might be argued, for example, that the quest narrative of *Star Wars* enables Lucas to incorporate contradictory discourses about femininity into his text (via the characterisation of Leia, use and representation of technology) without that amibiguity being apparent to viewers. If it is experienced at all, it is as humour, and that humour has a very conservative ideological basis. Moreover, the contradiction is thus experienced as an internal textual element, with the notion of the text as a site for the construction of meaning effectively concealed.

Mad Max 3 cannot be dismissed so easily. As Ross Gibson notes, Kennedy-Miller consistently display respect for the cinematic literacy of their audience:

> . . . *Mad Max Beyond Thunderdome* is also vitally concerned with storytelling. It has a narrativity that is made no less meaningful by the comic sense accompanying it. When the ringmaster of the Thunderdome turns to the camera to confide the artifice of it all directly to the audience, he can have no doubt that sooner or later everyone will know that this entire drama depends on the viewers' recognising the reenactments and the rhetorics from a myriad cinematic stories. Every sight and sound is carrying a message, and the film knows this; the film is about this telling, and it tells its watchers so.

It is interesting to note that the most consistent criticism of *Mad Max 3* by reviewers is that it is fragmented, most noticeably in the transition of Max from Bartertown to the Crack in the Earth. So in *Mad Max 3* the transformation fundamental to the narrative, where Max is shaken out of his apathy, is seen as clumsy, not invisibly stitched into the text. Given the optimism with which the narrative concludes, along with its scenes of the nuclear devastation of Sydney, this apparent fragmentation of the narrative is very interesting. What it highlights, and what the text constantly represents, is that this is a narrative about storytelling, a narrative that constantly refers to its own practice, as it does in the overdetermined collection of generic images by which Max is constructed at the beginning of the film.

Faultless Fragmentation: Soap Opera

By comparison, I want to consider briefly a genre notorious for its apparent realism and its ability to persuade viewers of that realism. You might think I am going to discuss the 'news', but I simply refer you to the work of the Glasgow Media Studies Group on that subject. Actually I want to consider 'soap opera'. Without taking on the whole of the current debate about soap opera (see Ang, Docker, Modleski, Tulloch), I want to make a few basic points about these extraordinary texts. Soap operas are usually presented as texts that invite close identification with characters, that inveigle viewers into a naive acceptance of narrative. Even the most concerned media critics seem to proceed from the basis that soap operas use a consistent narrative that is productive of meanings either inimical to or supportive of minority views or rights. In Masterman's terms, they judge the soap opera 'because of (its) "bias" or the suppression or demotion of alternative viewpoints'. And I certainly think there is a place for such analysis. However, if it is devoid of awareness of the textuality of the text, again in Masterman's words, of the 'notion of the text as a site for the construction of meanings', then the analysis of the text could be extremely misleading.

With soap operas, for example, it seems to me that the conventions of the genre itself often conflict with the naturalising function of the narrative. These conventions are often so bizarre, so outrageously unrealistic, that they rupture (that is, break in a noticeable and decisive way) the realist surface of the narrative. The conventions include memory loss (where a character disappears from a soapie only to reappear up to a year or more later after suffering loss of memory); the double (where a character acting uncharacteristically or so badly as to require — realistically — imprisonment or hospitalisation is found to be the long-lost evil twin of the regular); actor replacement (when a new actor takes on the role of a regular without apology — and sometimes when the 'old' regular is brought back due to public demand); plastic surgery (when a new actor takes on the role of a regular, with apology); the dream (when a long section of the soapie is made redundant by the revelation that it was all a dream by one of the regulars, used flamboyantly in *Dallas* to resurrect a popular regular, Bobby Ewing); temporal inconsistency (it has been calculated that Dr Tom Horton of *Days of Our Lives* is over 160 years old); and impossibly complex interrelationships (most characters in soapies are either related or married or have slept together, and in celebrated instances, all three). The question that has to be addressed here is whether the constant rupturing of the narrative realism does call attention to the fictionality of the soapie, the same question that needs to be asked of *Mad Max 3*. Furthermore, even when the audience does recognise the text as process rather than product, are they also aware of the implications of this process? Are they aware of the text as a site for the production of meanings?

The self-referentiality of many contemporary texts suggests that the makers do respect the audience's literacy. They seem to accept that audiences do play with texts, that the pleasure of watching a soapie is not a simple acceptance of soapie conventions, but a learned ability to play with those conventions, to guess at the development of the narrative by reference to those conventions, fantastic as they often are. But do audiences thereby become aware of issues of narrativity, of the manufacture of texts, including news and current affairs as well as the more overtly fictional genres? This is an issue the critic must confront as a component of the analysis of any film or television text. It should inform, though not necessarily dominate, the analysis.

I have discussed the concepts of narrative and genre, the ideological assumptions, practices and discourses that operate within these basic elements of textual production. And I have referred them to several well-known texts, primarily *Star Wars* and *Mad Max Beyond Thunderdome* as examples of the kind of textual analysis they necessitate. However, I have not been able to deal at length with the many economic determinants that are crucial in the production of film and television texts. Let me leave you with just some of them; leave you to integrate them into your analysis of a text:

- movie backers, the people who supply the money, often insist that well-known 'stars' be included in the cast before they will finance a film;
- movie backers may also insist that particular elements be included in a plot (for instance, more sex, more violence);
- movie backers may demand a well-known director be employed, who can be trusted to bring the film in on time and within budget;

Boy George: character as soap opera; constant disruption of narrative surface, generic convention

- the major cinema audience is the late child/early adolescent age group;
- children and adolescents avoid 'G' rated films like the plague;
- film advertising may be an important element in the pre-construction of a film by its audience;
- modern cinemas are often noisy, television having disrupted the silence convention learned from 'live' theatre attendance, at least for certain categories of film;
- cinema owners earn a large percentage of their revenue from the sale of confectionery and other attractions such as video games;
- television programs, at least in pilot form, are made for the executives of television studios;
- television programs are evaluated on their ability to attract advertisers;

- advertising rates change according to the time of day, that is, according to the characteristics of the potential audience;
- television programs are often interrupted by and edited for advertisements;
- some television programs, especially for children, are produced specifically to sell commercial products;
- television audiences rarely watch the screen without being involved in other activities at the same time;
- television advertisers have already demanded reduced rates because of the viewer practice of zapping, that is, recording programs on video and fast-forwarding through the advertisements.

This list could and should be extended. I hope I have indicated some of the issues it should include and their potential effects on the text.

We as textual critics must be fundamentally concerned with the issues I have raised at length, to do with the production of a visual representation of the 'real', the viewing position(s) produced by those representations and possible subversions of them often contained within the same text, and the status of those texts in relation to the social formation of which they are at once product, process, expression and reinforcement. Through this analysis we can reach some understanding of the significance and meaning of a text. As critics we must integrate awareness of issues such as financial determinants, production practices and audience expectation into this analysis, particularly if we are to move beyond the stage of analysis to an active intervention in the industries that are so crucial to our society today.

Further Reading

Ang, Ien *Watching Dallas: Soap opera and the melodramatic imagination* Tr D Couling Methuen 1985

De Lauretis, Teresa *Alice Doesn't: Feminism, Semiotics, Cinema* Macmillan 1984

Gibson, Ross, 'Yondering: A Reading of *Mad Max Beyond Thunderdome*'. Art & Text 19 1985

Heath, Stephen *Questions of Cinema* Macmillan, 1981

Kress, Gunther *Linguistic processes in sociocultural practice* Deakin University Press 1985

Kuhn, Annette *The power of the image: Essays on representation and sexuality* Routledge & Kegan Paul 1985

Masterman, Len 'Media Education: Theoretical Issues and Practical Possibilities' Metro 60 1983

Mathews, Sue *35mm Dreams* Penguin 1984

Modleski, Tania *Loving with a Vengeance: Mass-Produced Fantasies for Women* Methuen 1982

Neale, Steve *Genre* BFI London.1980
Tulloch, John and Manuel Alvarado *Doctor Who: The Unfolding Text* Macmillan
   1983

GLOSSARY OF TERMS

This glossary sets out some terms that might be most immediately problematic for readers. It is by no means exhausting, and is not meant to be. Difficult terms, whether listed here or not, should be looked up in the index and read in their contexts. This will usually give a better sense of the meaning or use of a term in this book.

Absence The term points to two aspects of meaning. One is that the act of not mentioning something that might have been mentioned is meaningful; it might be a sign of the suppression of meaning. The other is that meaning exists out of a contrast of what is 'there' and what is not there: the patterning of the Eiffel Tower is a factor of the interplay of the pieces of the structure that are present — girders, platforms — with the empty enclosed spaces.

Bureaucracy A term that refers to the group of administrative, technical, and clerical workers in private business and the public services; and the set of practices and relations developed by them in the carrying out of their functions.

Capitalism The system of ownership of the means of production other than labour. *Capital* is the stock of accumulated wealth that can be applied to the task of producing goods and services.

Class In Marxist sociology the term describes a group whose members occupy a common economic position and who hold a shared consciousness of their social and economic position. This definition differs from others that do not consider consciousness but use general quantitative or positional criteria such as income or status.

Closure The process that brings about, for the reader or viewer, the sense of completeness of a structure, a process that actively engages the reader's participation as the one who brings about closures.

Code The systematic organisation of elements in a particular medium of communication for the purposes of effective communication. Codes have to be shared by a group in order to function. The organisation of the code reflects crucial aspects of the social situation in which the code functions.

Communication The term encompasses the complex, socially located processes and structures of the production, transmission and reproduction/reception of meaning. It is a process performed by social agents which involves salient cultural values and social structures in the reproduction of existent, or the production of new, meaning.

Connotation The set of meanings that cluster around the central meaning of a term and are brought into play whenever the central meaning is invoked. *See* denotation.

Control The term refers to the action of particular agents in attempting to regulate the behaviour and practices of (themselves and) others, directly or indirectly, for instance via the establishment of written or unwritten rules.

Convention The term points to the idea of a socially established and generally unspoken agreement of historical standing about the performance of specific social practices, ranging from 'acceptable' ways of eating peas to ways of conducting warfare — as set out in the 'Geneva Convention'.

Culture The term refers to the set of human practices that produce meaning and to the objects that are the result of those practices. It encompasses all forms of human engagement in those practices, and their effects on humans acting together as a 'culture'.

Denotation The core or central meaning of a term.

Dialogic process The term refers to the idea that all texts, even those ostensibly by a single author, are the result of many 'voices', coming from the differing social groups of which any one society is composed and which are brought into dialogue with the voice of a speaker or writer. Hence all meaning-making activity is seen not as the product of a single author's expressive act, but as the expression of a multiplicity of voices mediated by one author.

Discourse Systematically organised ways of talking, which give expression to the values and meaning of particular institutions.

Gender A profoundly important organising principle in social life, based, in the first instance, on biological differences and dualities in human reproduction. In all human societies these differences have been drawn into culture in particular ways, and revalued in line with other economic, material, and social principles of organisation.

Genre A kind of text that derives its form from the structure of a (frequently repeated) social occasion, with its characteristic participants and their purposes. Because such texts are often repeated, the form takes on (the appearance of) a certain autonomy as a merely formal category.

Ideology A notoriously difficult term, with at least the following core-meanings: the system of values, beliefs, crucial practices of a particular group; a mistaken set of beliefs, values, or a false theory held by a group; a set of beliefs, values, practices imposed by one group on another in order to further its own ends. This last, the Marxist use, leads to the notion of false consciousness.

Intertextuality This refers to two complementary ideas. First, that all producers of texts draw on the existence of other texts, contemporaneous or prior, in the production of 'their' text, so that texts are constructs made of strands of other texts. Second, in doing so, the significance of the new text is augmented by the significance of all texts that form a part of it, so that each text is the central point of a far-reaching web of meaning. Reading is seen as intertextual also, an activity in which readers draw on their knowledge of prior texts in the reading/reconstruction of any particular text.

Kinship The term kinship is used to refer to the ties that exist between those who are seen as related, either through birth or marriage. It is a social means of organising and regulating sexuality, assigning parentage and transferring rights and duties from one generation to another. Kinship relates to the ways in which human reproduction is socially understood.

Language The most fully articulated of all media of human communication. All societies have language in the spoken form. In literate societies language in the written and in the spoken modes are organised in significantly different ways, and have different social uses and valuations. Language is a socio-cultural construct, encoding cultural values; it is constantly deployed in the production and reproduction of social and cultural values.

Meaning A relational term that indicates a number of factors in a complex relationship between social individuals and the systems of practices and values to which they subscribe. The term refers to the whole vast complex of objects and relations, concrete and abstract, human and non-human, that are culturally relevant, i.e. that have been made relevant in a culture. 'Meaning' refers to a particular item in that complex, or to a set of relations, and to the place it has for a particular individual, to the congruence of discrepancy between the place of an object in one individual's system compared to that of another.

Metaphor The term initially describes the process of transference of a quality or meaning from one item to another. It then becomes used frequently as a description of the item to which the quality or meaning has been transferred. At times the metaphor is obvious; 'He's as bright as a button'; more frequently it is more implicit: 'Things are looking up' where the quality of animateness has been transferred from animate objects to inanimate things, and where 'up' has been recipient of the meanings 'positive, optimistic, good'. Metaphor is pervasive and fundamental to all language use: this last clause is made up (a metaphor) of several metaphors.

Metonym This involves the displacement of meaning from a whole larger item or structure to a part, the part can then signify the whole. The flag as a symbol of everything that a nation 'stands for' is one example. 'Giving your hand in marriage' is another.

Myth The narrative organisation of culturally salient material into accounts that have a pervasive and telling effect, summing and compressing complex experience into readily assimilable form. Anecdotes are small-scale examples of mythic structure. 'How the West was won' in America, or 'Stories of the Outback' in Australia are larger level versions. At times, vastly complex mythic structures are compressed into a single symbol, such as 'The Rock', the figure of the drover on his horse, the Sydney Harbour Bridge, the Digger's slouch hat.

Narrative The sequenced structuring and presentation of culturally significant material which inevitably involves conflict and transformation. Narrative tends to have a structure of initial equilibrium — disturbance of the equilibrium — resolution of the disturbance — equilibrium. In the course of the narrative, troublesome issues may be assimilated; due to the return to an equilibrium, narrative structures are inherently conservative in their ideological effect.

Networking The organisation of television stations into groups that function to purchase programs or organise program-making for all the stations in the 'network'.

Power The term refers to relationships between groups or individuals, directly or mediated via cultural constructs such as (the texts of) rules, regulations, laws, with the focus on the possibilities of one group or one individual forcing others into certain actions, practices, or the desisting from actions; and the obverse, the possibility of resistance to such force.

Reader Position Every text, whether an image, a film, or a verbal text, constructs a position from which it should ideally be read or viewed. From that position the text will seem unproblematic, natural.

Segmentation The creation of separate media, and media outlets designed for a particular 'market segment'. Segmentation occurs within one medium, as when television schedules programs for a specific market segment at a particular time of the day. Segmentation is an aid in delivering audiences as potential consumers to advertisers.

Sentence The crucial syntactic and textual unit of written language. Typically, the sentence is characterised by an internal hierarchical structuring of clauses which metaphorically represents the structuring of meaning in the sentence.

Sign A conjunction of a signifier and a signified, a formal element and an element of meaning. In traditional discussions it is assumed that the conjunction is arbitrary and conventional. In more recent discussions it is increasingly assumed that signifier and signified are not arbitrarily related, but rather that there is a strong social motivation for their conjunction.

Speech The medium in which language is common to all humans, barring certain pathological conditions. Speech is however not 'natural', that is, it is entirely a cultural construct, and consequently embodies social and cultural meanings everywhere in its form.

State That constellation of institutions whose function it is to govern: the parliament, the public service, courts, prisons, police, the military, the secret intelligence services.

Structure This term points to an assumption that all socio-cultural systems are organised in particular ways, as a (usually finite) set of terms, with a specified set of relations between them. Structure exists in the paradigmatic plane, where terms occur in organised systems, and in the syntagmatic plane, where terms chosen from the system are put into an organised sequential form.

Text The term describes the unit that results from a completed act of communication, in any medium of communication. Texts are the material expressions of meanings of various origin brought together in one place by the maker of the text. They are therefore always the effect of the action of social forces at work in communication.

Writing The medium in which language is available to literate groups.

Like speech, writing is an entirely cultural activity, and therefore has particular cultural uses and cultural meanings. Access to writing and to its various forms is distributed along lines of social power in any society.

INDEX